Boost Your Bullsh*t Resilience At Work

Escape the Cesspool with 13 Transformative Approaches

Chris Reavis

thebsbook.com

YFH Publishing

Avid Intent LLC

PO Box 1962

Wilsonville, OR 97070 USA

COPYRIGHT @2024 Chris Reavis

Published by YFH Publishing, a division of Avid Intent LLC.

All rights reserved. This book or parts of it may not be reproduced in any form, stored in any retrieval system, or transmitted in any form by any means - electronic, mechanical, photocopy, recording, or otherwise - without prior written permission of the publisher, except as provided by United States of America copyright law.

ISBNs: 978-1-7378538-5-5 (paperback), 978-1-7378538-2-4 (eBook)

Library of Congress Control Number: 2024903462

First Edition

By reading this document, the reader agrees that under no circumstances is the author or the publisher responsible for any losses, direct or indirect, which are incurred because of the use of information within this document, including but not limited to errors, omissions or inaccuracies.

Legal Notice:

This book is copyright-protected. Please note the information within this document is for education and personal use only. You cannot amend, distribute, sell, use, quote or paraphrase any part of the content within this book without the consent of the author or publisher.

For the mavericks, the altruists, the creatives, the action-takers, the jokers, the innovators, and the lovers!

If you haven't already, check out
our workbook and other goodies here.

Use your smartphone's camera to use the QR code above, or just go
to thebsbook.com/workbook.

Contents

Preface 1

Chapter 1: Boom 7

Chapter 2: Everyone Has A BS Work Story 11

Chapter 3: No Tolerance Bullsh*t 17

Section One: Why Bother? 23

Chapter 4: Impacts of Stressors 25
    Chapter Activity 29

Chapter 5: The Story of Two 12s 31

Chapter 6: Death By Meeting 35

Section Two: Is it time to leave? 41

Chapter 7: Time To Say Goodbye 43
    Are you ready to leave? 45
    Exit Stage Left - Your Checklist 50
    What To Expect If You Are Expecting 50

Section Three: Are Side Hustles for you? 55

Chapter 8: Side Hustles 57
    Wax On Wax Off 58
    Beware of The Seductive Sales Cycles 62
    Side Hustle Assessment 64
    Scoring Your Results 67

Section Four: What matters most? 69

Chapter 9: Your Goals and Why 71

Your Why Exercise 76
Chapter 10: Who Do You Want To Be 79
    Message to You Rudy 79
Chapter 11: What Should Your Work Life Look Like? 85
Section Five: BS Issues and Skills 93
Chapter 12: Skills You Can Build 95
Chapter 13: BS Issue - Waste 99
    Customer Empathy 99
    Meeting Waste 100
    Report Waste 101
Chapter 14: Skill - Smash 105
Chapter 15: BS Issue - Group Think 111
Chapter 16: Skill - Curiosity 117
Chapter 17: BS Issue - Problem Admiration 121
Chapter 18: Skill - Speak With Purpose 129
Chapter 19: BS Issue – Risk As An Excuse 137
Chapter 20: Skill - Plot Your Trajectory 147
    Course of Action and Manifesting 150
Chapter 21: BS Issue - Toxic Hero Culture 157
Chapter 22: Skill - Exercise 163
Chapter 23: BS Issue - Me Me Me 167
Chapter 24: Skill - Vent 175
Chapter 25: BS Issue - Shiny Object Syndrome 181

Chapter 26: Skill - Shiny Object Syndrome 189

Chapter 27: BS Issue - Wrongful Accusation 195

Chapter 28: Skill - This is It 203

Chapter 29: BS Issue - Yes-people and Brown-nosers 205

Chapter 30: Skill - Meditation and Visualization 213

Chapter 31: BS Issue - Over Celebrating 221

Chapter 32: Skill - Get Others to Problem Solve 227

Chapter 33: BS Issue - Excuses 235
    Chapter Exercise 239

Chapter 34: Skill - Follow the Customer 241

Chapter 35: BS Issue - Ethical Issues 247

Chapter 36: Skill - Draw a Picture and Use Insights 251
    Drawing The Picture 251
    Lights, Camera Action 253
    Get Insightful 254

Chapter 37: BS Issue - Pretending It's Okay 259

Chapter 38: Skill - Networking In the Clicky Clicky Age 263

Chapter 39: Skill – Confront the BS Head On 269
    FBI 270
    OTFD 272
    CPS 275
    Wrapping Up 279

Section Six: How do you use this? 281

Chapter 40: Formulas and Tools 283

Just Winging It 285
Chapter 41: Are You The Asshole? 287
Chapter 42: Best Practices for BS Reduction Routines 291
Chapter 43: Congratulations! 295
Bibliography 301

Preface

We spend nearly half our adult life at work.

Our work is also not just contained in our working hours. We fixate about our work and talk about work issues all the time – especially the bullshit ones.

We often bring that work stress home and into our relationships. It's easy at times to feel stuck. We repeat our stories and beliefs about our jobs.

In addition to our own personal work BS stories, we often catalog those of our friends and colleagues. We may laugh at the many movies and TV series that poke fun at the absurdity of what happens at so many offices. At times, though, it is just not funny. We are pissed, exhausted, frustrated, and angry. This feeling can stick with us and, even worse, take a major health toll. It's exhausting.

While we might write off some work BS to being just how it is, and we somewhat cope with it, others didn't get that memo. They don't have the skills to handle what we consider normal work BS. Just why are they whining so much, and why don't they get over it?

For some, I know, it seems like your workplace should owe you a lot and is not stepping up to honor how important and special you are.

Maybe you feel stuck in your job, hopeless and demeaned. You go into work like a robot and do your tasks on autopilot. You may have given up on things ever being different at work. You know you must make the money for housing, a car, and your family – and you plod along in survival mode at work.

Fortunately, you don't have to put up with all this workplace BS. You can also build up your BS tolerance through a set of skills. This mix of skills can help you through the trickiest of situations. You also do not have to settle for crap, and these skills also help eliminate BS instead of you having to keep wading through it.

Through several common situations and stories, this book will walk you through practical, evidence-based ways to create change. While I did keep some of this funny (as it's good to laugh), much of it is also serious because it is your life. Like me, many of you will be skeptical about some of these skills and may say to yourself, "WTF, Chris?" That's okay!

While I've made more than my share of career mistakes and don't even pretend to be the poster child for corporate success, I've also been exposed to some gems. These gems got me through the most gnarly work situations. All gems mentioned here also have an evidence base, so it's not just another set of empty "feel good, be positive" solutions. So, what kind of jobs have I had, and would this experience even relate to yours? Well, I've had every color collar of jobs there is in my career, including:

- Church janitor (thousands of people can make a mess)
- Fast food (queue the polyester and zits)
- Envelope stuffing (so glamorous)
- Telemarketing (or hang-up management)
- Camp counselor (want to hear some songs?)
- Pre-press scanner operator (night shift 6 days a week)

- College computer lab tech ("You mean I shouldn't use my floppy as a coffee coaster for my master's thesis?"
- Door-to-door sales (before Ring devices)
- Software developer (I was pretty awful at this)
- Infrastructure administrator (I was better at this)
- Project manager (I despised this)
- Professional services manager (dances with billable hours)
- Software sales (very short-lived)
- Landlord (rent's due!)
- Technical architect (boxes, arrows, and lots of politics)
- IT Director (sometimes fancy, but rarely, with lots of late nights and weekends)
- Drop shipping (glad I dropped this side hustle)
- Car Detailer (side hustle you'll hear about)
- Internet marketing (another side hustle)
- Bitcoin miner (still am)
- Online course builder (more to come here!)
- Parent Coach (attempting to undo bad habits from well-intentioned people)
- Non-profit board member (awesome opportunities to serve)
- Author (which you probably knew!)

It's a big list, and every one of them needed a different type of resilience for those special days – and sometime months. I learned that no matter how bleak the situation feels now, there are options and actions you can take. It will take repeated efforts and will not be instant. You may need to make changes. Some of these are simple.

What's especially important to remember here is that the brilliance of your contributions is needed. You owe it to yourself to share them. Yes, the BS will come up and, at times, be overwhelming. However, you can master handling this and keep moving forward. You are always bigger than the BS you are experiencing.

This book is structured to help you get the very best outcomes, no matter what you are up against right now. Here are the six sections of the book.

Section One: Why Bother?

Learn the impacts of work stressors on your life and how it impacts your physical health.

Section Two: Is it time to leave?

If it really is that time, know the best steps to take to benefit you long-term.

Section Three: Are Side Hustles for you?

Explore what may and may not make sense for you.

Section Four: What matters most?

Understand your unique guiding principles and what matters most to you.

Section Five: BS Issues and Skills

Enjoy 13 proven skills to overcome BS, along with help identifying BS patterns.

Section Six: How do you use this?

Understand how to best apply what you have learned for your success.

For my fellow rule-breakers who like to jump around, know that this is your book to use as you like. So, if that is you, jump away! Many of you may also read through things once and later pop back to them as a reference. That's a great pattern, too. Whether you are a rule follower or maverick, please invest some time in the "your why" exercises in Section Four. So many of us skip-over work like this… and then wonder why the same crap keeps following us around. These exercises can help get rid of the poo following you around at every job you take, so they are worth it.

Thanks for making the investment in yourself, and enjoy the book!

CHAPTER 1

Boom

Margaret plodded into the office building like she had for decades. She somehow juggled her lunch, workout bag, negotiated badging in, and waved at her co-workers as she plodded over to her cube.

Margaret had done this job for over 15 years. While it was often demeaning, she thought it was the best she could do for herself. She put up with a lot of BS because of that decision. She hoped to retire in a few years.

Before she could get settled, her boss ordered her to come to his office. He always did this loudly over the cubes. It always embarrassed her and made her feel small. She worked hard to do the right thing.

After his summoning, all the cubes went silent. Many quietly expressed sympathy for Margaret. Others wondered why she put up with this. All of them were glad they were not the target of the tyrant bosses yelling this morning.

Through the closed door, they could hear the boss in muffled tones upset about something. After his outburst, Margaret shuffled back out of his office and began to head back to her cube.

But then, boom.

Everything blurred out for Margaret.

"What was that?"

"Did you hear that?"

"OMG, Margaret, are you okay!?"

Margaret found herself on the floor. She could hear people but could not answer. Her chest was tight. She could barely breathe. She could hardly move.

"Call 911!" she heard someone yell.

She faded out again.

Margaret kept fading in and out of consciousness during the ambulance ride to the hospital. She worried about her husband, kids and grandkids. She needed to call them. She would be late to the grandkids' school play. She tried to say this, but no words came out, and she passed out again.

She later woke up in the hospital with beeps, lights and nurses looking frightened when they saw her. They were yelling something at her, but she couldn't respond. She tried to wave her hand. She was not sure if it moved at all.

Before she faded out again, she understood that she was headed into surgery.

Later, as she came to, she heard her husband and kids, or at least she thought it was them. She hurt all over. She caught a glimpse of her favorite tulips. As she tried to inhale and talk, everything burned badly.

Suddenly, a machine next to her beeped loudly, and three nurses rushed in. A crash cart was rushed in, and she felt her body flop as the charges hit her.

Margaret faded out for the last time. She tried to contact her family, but her body didn't move anymore.

Margaret knew it was her time to go now. She wanted to say goodbye to her family but could not anymore. She wished she could tell them she loved them just one more time.

Out of nowhere, she also worried about her lunch going bad. Would someone put it in the fridge?

She laughed gently to herself as a bright light calmed her.

...

While Margaret's story is fictional, it is sadly not far from the truth. Research from all over the world has connected ongoing work BS (aka work stress) with cardiovascular disease:

- Harvard researchers found in a global study that "work is highly stressful have a 40% increased risk of heart disease (including heart attacks and the need for coronary artery surgery) compared with their less-stressed colleagues." (1)
- The American Heart Association showed that "women who worry about losing their jobs are more likely to have high blood pressure and unhealthy cholesterol levels and to be obese." (7)
- In Europe, a large 15-year study showed that the greater the work pressure, the higher the risk for heart disease." (3)
- In Asia, a study found the same pattern: "white-collar workers in Beijing, job strain was associated in women (but not in men) with increased thickness of the carotid artery wall, an early sign of cardiovascular disease." (4)

In addition to our physical and mental health, the stress of BS work environments can result in our threat mechanisms always being on. This system is useful in life-or-death situations but not designed to be always on. "When the fight-or-flight response is chronically in the "on" position, the body suffers." (5)

So, there is much more impact on your health from work BS situations than you might think. Like Margaret, unchecked, you could lose your life because of work BS. As it turns out, pretending that everything is fine is not a strategy that works. Even if it doesn't go as far as to take your life, the moments spent dealing with work BS are not ones you can get back later.

So, let's make sure that your work BS doesn't make you another statistic and instead give you some proven strategies to succeed!

CHAPTER 2

Everyone Has A BS Work Story

"You'll never guess what happened to me today at work…"

That story continues with something like, "My boss said this and did that, and I didn't like it." Or "They did this to us." Or "So and so was stinky again and did this."

Does that sound familiar?

How many times *this week* have you said it?

And, if you didn't say it this week, how many times have you heard it this week?

While I am not aware of any statistics of this being a common conversation topic, most of us can identify with hearing this often. Whether it is at a happy hour, on social media, with friends, or with family - we talk about BS at work.

Usually, this has the theme of being something we consider dumb, something that hinders us, or something that repeatedly occurs.

Let's be honest - most of us have a BS at work story - if not a few dozen. We may even have favorites.

In this book, we'll share a number of situations that might seem incredibly similar to what you may be going through. However, we will not join the commiserating of the Bullshit. Sorry, not sorry.

Oh sure, we will acknowledge that it's there - no doubt. BS at work is probably at an all-time high. Instead of commiserating, this book will work to help you know what to wade through (eww), what to escape from (run Forrest run), and sometimes even how to be Teflon so it doesn't get to you at all.

Sound good?

Many of us may expect work to be filled with BS. Others may be unknowingly creating a small mountain of BS for others. At the same time, we may also start getting used to a solid serving of BS in our lives. This can quietly be making the load on our lives and our ability to cope much more intolerable.

This is not a "tough love" book. If you could have gotten over it already, you already would have. Actually, the brain science there is clear. We'll get to that later.

Instead of thinking you should get over it, what might be needed are new skills and tools to navigate the shit creek. In this analogy, this book could even be the paddle for you.

Bad Dad jokes aside, the intention here is to help. To do that, there are exercises at the end of most chapters and a companion workbook to help you get the most out of this journey. Here are three ways you can use this book successfully:

1. Scan through this book, don't do any exercises or self-reflection, and be surprised that not much changes in the BS department at work.
2. Read some of the book, do an exercise or two, be a little honest with yourself about the hard stuff, and get a small amount of change.

3. Read the book. Be brave and do the exercises (and perhaps also the workbook). Be honest with yourself about what's going on. Attempt some of the tools in a few situations. Enjoy some lasting change and benefits.

No matter the level, you want to engage in BS remediation and skill building, this book is here for you. And to be honest, I've done all three of these approaches with many books - more often than not, in the first two camps. I will not try to BS you and tell you otherwise!

It turns out that being brave to take action and make changes actually goes against our core programming. Aside from engaging our threat mechanisms and change feeling like more work, our primitive survival mechanisms will create many reasons *not to act*. If it is currently "working" - even if it's painful, sad, gross or stinky - it's known. In this program, knowing equals safety and good. Staying safe means the preservation of the species. This is really helpful programming to stay away from predators and served us well in early times. But, in today's workplace, the likelihood of literally being eaten alive is rare. Oh, it can feel like that, and we may even say those words. What's interesting is that even though these are dramatically different situations, our brain perceives the threats the same, even though a saber tooth monster isn't stalking us.

So, fortunately, you are not lunch for another creature anymore. However, your brain may fight new ideas with the good intention of keeping you from being a snack. So, as you read this book, if a "no way that's going to work" comes up, notice if it's the "I'm going to be a snack" program coming up. Our brain stem is exceptional at quickly deciding things that are fight or flight moments, and it is a gatekeeper for other parts of the brain. It is super scary fast at doing this - and those decisions can be made before we know it.

Wait a second, what's all this brain stuff and talking about me? Isn't this book about them? They are doing this to me at work. Those BSers are creating this. I'm perfect (or close to it) and need others to change. If they stopped or went away, everything would be fine, right?

Maybe.

And maybe, just maybe, there are a few skills you can build up to handle the BS that's likely to occur throughout your career. The nice thing about books and journals like this is that you get to be honest with yourself. You don't have to pretend that you are someone else to fit in or emulate any norms of society. If you want to drop the F bomb, drop it. If you want to scream (in your hand might be smart from a noise perspective), scream. If you want to admit some things are horrid - do so.

You are among friends here, and everyone I know has made good and bad decisions in their careers. All are still alive and haven't become snacks. Some "put up" with BS by stuffing it away and pretending it's not a big deal. This usually takes a massive toll on their health and families. It also doesn't respond well to alcohol and drugs. It makes the BS worse and sticky. Yeah, more eww.

Others may jump from job to job whenever the BS becomes too much. They don't yet have the skills to assess, handle or change what comes up. And it still keeps coming. It's still sticky (and still eww).

Sometimes, we can navigate what's coming up at work, maybe even change it, and change our demeanor around it.

Now, let's be clear: this isn't pretending - we acknowledge what's going on and how we feel about it. We also don't judge ourselves for being wimps for feeling that way. Then, after being honest, we apply a new skill. Like the BS, it's messy at first and takes time. However, when used with consistency, we don't have to hide, pretend or jump. This is a much healthier way to be, and life is frankly way too short to put up with BS any other way.

CHAPTER 3

No Tolerance Bullsh*t

It takes poop to grow, but too much of it is toxic and kills. Let's be clear - there are specific situations you should have no tolerance for. None. Zero.

These are not situations to apply these new skills and hope for change.

Sadly, sometimes, you must remove yourself for your safety, mental health and future. Even in our modern, evolved world, there are issues in the workplace.

In talking to my friends and co-workers, I'm astounded by stories from previous employers. It's like a textbook of what not to do - sexual harassment, discrimination, physical intimidation, severe cruelty, and so much more.

So, if you are involved in any of these situations, you need to be honest. If you are being abused at work - and you get to define what this means - and you experience this as an ongoing pattern, you likely will leave.

Here is where the "I'm going to be a snack" part of your brain comes in with fear. After reading this, you may be flooded with messages like "yeah, that's easy for you to say, you don't know…" or "I can't leave because I have to pay my rent and help my kids" or "there's no other job for me." Remember, you are not at risk of being a snack anymore. That program might not be serving you right now.

Now, you may choose to plan your exit and not to leap right away from this horrid situation. Sometimes, there could be timing involved that serves you best. You could have a bonus coming or know of a new job opening in a few weeks. If so, know that you are steering this choice and are not a victim. You are also not saying it's okay. You are timing things for your benefit.

My other recommendation here is that you document everything you can. Now, I don't mean taking confidential work products into your possession. However, you can keep an inventory of when issues happen, what they are, and who was involved. I hope you never have to do this, and it frankly can feel gross. I've had to do this at a few employers that were blatantly discriminatory. It can feel like you are keeping score, telling someone, or whining. You aren't. You also may be laying down the foundation so the people after you don't have to put up with the same. It's worth it.

When you are ready to leave and have an exit plan, I would recommend using whatever means your company provides to file a complaint. Often, there are anonymous phone lines or similar ways to do this. Some companies don't have these, so there's probably someone you can contact in Human Resources. Again, it's easy not to want to do this and just leave. And again, please remember you are probably helping others not deal with this after you. It's worth it.

Now, as much as your company may claim to be wonderful and inclusive, and maybe even won awards for being the best place to work, be prepared for some ugly here. While I hope this isn't true for you, the stories I hear from many around this are consistent. Companies seek to protect themselves from legal exposure in these situations. They may be empathetic and even share that they will do something. However, you will hear how busy they are and not see a lot of action. While I hope you prove me wrong and share an amazing story of how a company did the right thing, that's rare.

At a previous employer, I had an overt example of discrimination. For a long list of reasons, I'm not going into great detail on what happened. Please trust, for this situation, I had plenty of documentation, examples, and evidence. While there was some gray - it's not always clear - there were clear violations of both corporate policies and the law. I believed in the company and their ethos overall, and they have won many awards for being a great place to work. They also won awards for being inclusive to many people and had employee groups for support. So, what happened when I made my complaint was frankly stunning, given this environment and their awards.

When I was first very emotional about this, the HR person taking the complaint was empathetic. I had hoped they would come to my rescue and take action. They followed up a few days later to see if I was okay. They shared that they had a backlog and would do an investigation soon. Guess what? I touched base every few weeks for three months. The story was still about how busy they were. Translation - your case isn't important, and we hope you go away. Finally, after checking in for four months on a weekly basis, they assigned me to one of the internal lawyers to "help out."

While I was excited to finally share my story and begin the investigation, this session was also stunning. Looking back, I should have known better and had different expectations. Again, though, this was supposed to be an involved, inclusive workplace that wins awards for being so great. Fairly quickly into the conversation, I was being second-guessed and treated like the incidents had not happened. This is what I would expect in a trial if I was on the stand,

and I didn't have my own lawyer to yell "objection!" So, what did this internal lawyer offer as a resolution after this conversation? What was their big insight?

"Maybe things will get better."

Yes, really, that's what they said. Okay, not to carry this too far, but could you imagine saying this to someone suffering from domestic abuse? Yeah, that would be both dumb, not realistic, and not helpful. Someone in that situation needs help getting out of it, and the abuser needs to be dealt with to stop the pattern for others.

As you read this story, many of you will have a much more severe story or know someone who has. These are not isolated incidents.

So, while I do recommend that you document everything and follow the reporting process your company has, I don't recommend having high hopes for a movie-like outcome with theme music.

Usually, with these severe situations, you may need to plan on leaving the company. You can continue your fight after leaving, but staying in an oppressive situation where no change will be made is not a healthy choice.

I'm sorry that if you are dealing with this, you have to deal with this. It's awful. It's exhausting. You will second-guess yourself.

Two pieces of good news here:

1. You will get past it, and there are better places to be.
2. The skills in the rest of this book will help in other situations. They also may help you as you time your exit.

For everyone else, I'm glad you haven't had to deal with this, hope you never have to, and what's next will help you in the many situations you'll experience that aren't as severe.

22

SECTION ONE

Why Bother?

Learn the impacts of work stressors on your life and how it impacts your physical health.

CHAPTER 4

Impacts of Stressors

"If it ain't' broke, don't fix it…"

Adages like this may stop us from reflecting on what's going on for us. Sometimes we think we should be tough and endure, and what we experience at work is "nothing compared to what others experience." Sometimes, we think we can ignore it, and it will go away.

What's interesting is that part of our brain that still fears becoming a snack to a predator can act up here and be defensive as we seek healthier situations. As weird as that is, remember the current state - even if not healthy - is the known state and safe to this ancient brain programming. Anything else is considered dangerous – even healthier options.

As it turns out, lots of us are just putting up with it at work. A major study by Gallup, reported by the Harvard Business Review (6), found "that employees around the world are experiencing stress at an all-time-high level, and worry, anger, and sadness remain above pre-pandemic levels. These emotions are organizational risks: If leaders aren't paying attention to employee wellbeing, they're likely to be blindsided by top-performer burnout and high quit rates. Today's leaders must think beyond physical wellness to capture the broader dimensions of overall well-being, capture data on how their employees are doing, and make employee care a permanent part of organizational culture."

Our workplaces are more dynamic than ever, with a large mix of different age groups, belief systems and nationalities. We are all experiencing a new level of stressors at home, too, along with those at work.

Some workplaces will make mild attempts at employee wellbeing, mostly geared towards keeping their top performers from leaving. However, the data shows that there's a lot of work to still do here. This same Gallup research found "that fewer than one in four U.S. employees felt strongly that their employer cared about their wellbeing — the lowest percentage in nearly a decade."

This study shares that "44% of employees say they experienced a lot during the previous day."

What does that translate to? The amount of BS we are all carrying, just based on the workplace, is at an all-time high. While it may seem subtle, mild, and something you should just deal with, what it can do to our bodies and long-term health is significant.

Let's look at what this workplace BS we are enduring is doing to our health.

In the construction industry, a study from the University of Cape Town (2) found that:

- Most respondents experience *"high levels* of stress at work."
- Female architects experienced the most stress.
- Physical effects included "usual sleep patterns, difficulty in relaxing after hours, and difficulty in concentrating. Sociological effects include a strain on family life, social activities, and social relationships."

- Negative coping included "consumption of alcohol is widespread, with more than one-third of respondents consuming 3–9 units/week. One in six respondents report smoking up to 40 cigarettes/day, whereas use of narcotics (such as marijuana, cocaine, mandrax, ecstasy, heroin, and methamphetamine) at least once in the previous 12 months is reported by 1 in 20."

Okay, maybe you aren't in construction, and maybe you don't work in a developing country, but do these effects resonate at all? Our brain wiring doesn't care if something should be easier or harder - it just experiences the stress event. If your brain interprets an event as a fight/flight/freeze event, the threat response modules are activated - like if you were about to be that snack to a bear.

Yes, I know that sounds silly - as hopefully there's no bear about to eat you in your everyday life - that would be a bit beyond the coping skills we will cover later. It is just as silly to judge your stress as "not big" while your body reacts to it and affects your life in larger ways than you could be acknowledging.

What does science show happen with these stressors we think we just have to put up with and get over? A lot.

In a research brief by the Iowa Department of Public Health (8), Dr. Bruce McEwen shares that "prolonged exposure to physiological or psychological stress results in over-use or overactivation of the brain's stress response and mediation systems."

When we experience these events - whatever our brains believe is a fight/flight/freeze event - cortisol and adrenaline flow. At the same time, the gateway to higher functions in our cerebral cortex is effectively shut off. We don't have reasoning, imagination, and calmness as options anymore. This is why when someone says something like "they are so mad that they cannot see straight" they could be right. Their brain has shut off other functions to deal with the stressor.

Let's be clear, there can be positive stressors that don't rise to the notion of work BS that are things we can find healthy coping mechanisms for. The goal here isn't to remove all stressors. However, we should be honest about the impacts of not dealing with our workplace BS.

The University of Massachusetts Lowell (9) found that toxic stressors - yes, the BS stuff - greatly increase the risk for:

- High cholesterol
- High blood pressure
- High blood sugar
- Weakened immune response.
- High cortisol
- Changes in appetite and digestive pattern

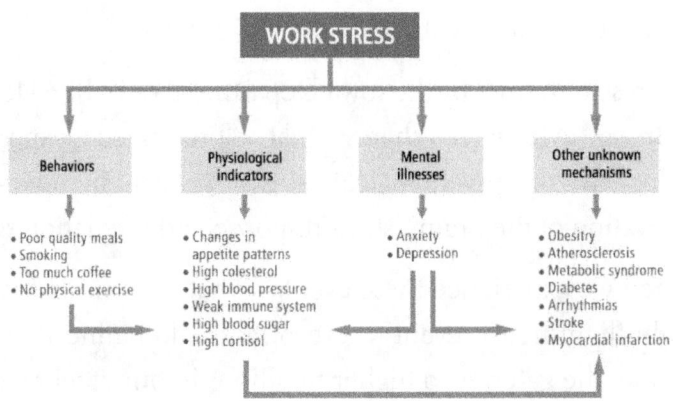

They share this diagram in their materials about the world that work stress creates. It spills into how we eat, what we may overindulge in, and things as severe as stroke.

Unattended to, this is what workplace BS can lead to. It cannot be ignored. Fortunately, there are some straightforward ways we can improve our everyday lives here that we will cover later in the skills section.

Chapter Activity

1. For a moment, pause and take a few deep breaths. This short exercise won't take long, don't worry! Okay, after reading this, close your eyes and imagine having no BS in your workday. That person who annoys you in meetings - they don't anymore. Imagine the busy work that makes no sense has disappeared. Anything that you consider BS - no matter how small or large - imagine that it's gone. Stay with this for a couple of minutes, then come back.

2. Do a quick reflection here - what were the 5-10 things that you'd want to see changed? Did this give you other ideas? Was it easy or hard to imagine these? Did you feel silly and like you should get over it? Did you notice more or less anxiety as you considered what you'd want to change?

3. After reading this chapter, do you notice anything that you might attribute to workplace stress? Are you emotionally eating a treat or two because "you deserve it"? Are you unwinding with more glasses of wine or bourbon than usual? Do you find your reserves are depleted and you have less ability to be with family and friends? It's okay to be honest

about these factors and judge them - what's going on for you right now?

CHAPTER 5

The Story of Two 12s

"Crap, did you hear that?" buzzed the assembly floor that morning. Dim, flickering blue, fluorescent lights buzzed overhead in the massive space where we spent so many hours. Much like Vegas, you couldn't tell if it was day or night because there were no windows. The drabness of the place was mirrored in our facial expressions. You could tell we all felt blah. Noises of machinery and people yelling out status of key jobs filled the air as we mindlessly went about our work.

We heard there was a new general manager, and so there was also lots of fear buzzing about what they might do. Many stories were passing around about how this GM invested in all sorts of nefarious things and was a tyrant, not to be messed with.

Most of us have never conversed with this person. He also hadn't talked to us on "the floor" before either. So, we were apt to believe whatever story we heard about him.

Soon, we were lined up to talk to the shop foreman and the new GM one by one. Many of us expected a layoff. Our loud and busy workplace became dead quiet.

It was so quiet that the speaker in the ceiling, which we thought was broken, was playing Muzak. It's the first time many of us have heard this. It attempted to squeak out the old tune "Danke Schoen" in a way both pathetic and sad.

Nobody said anything as they came out after their meeting with the new leaders, continuing the mystery. However, most went back to work, which seemed like a good sign. Nobody left with a pink folder, but the blank looks on their faces were still frightening.

My turn in line came. "Chris, have a seat". I'm not sure that I was breathing as I collapsed in the plastic chair. "Chris, I need you to work two twelves this weekend. We have a lot of work and need to catch up."

Now, as a backstory, we didn't have any more work to catch up on. I worked in pre-press as a scanner operator. Back in the 80s and 90s, things like Photoshop and digital editing didn't exist. For images to appear in a magazine, they had to be scanned in, retouched, and then type was hand laid out on each page.

Our work was done after the magazine finished their production and before press time. Press time is expensive, and a magazine's productions were often late getting to us. We were caught in the middle, so everything was always urgent. The shop ran 24/7/365 with two or three shifts.

I worked the swing/night shift. Because it was quieter then, as normal people were sleeping, we had high productivity. It wasn't unusual for me to do 90-120 scans in a shift, compared to maybe 20 on the day shift.

Okay, back to our story. I, perhaps luckily, had an out. I had a family visiting from out of town and had requested time off that weekend (we normally worked 6 days a week).

I offered the GM, "Could I work extra hours this week or do two twelves next weekend?" He paused. I was supposed to say yes or no to this shift request. He gave me a long hard look. I panicked again and imagined him firing me. I'd never been fired before.

"Chris, I didn't know that. I appreciate your offer. We'll get back to you. Go back to work."

I finished my 10-hour shift, and several others, not knowing my fate. I contemplated telling my family that, while they flew four hours to see me, I might not be available. On the Friday shift before this weekend, my boss said, "You're off the hook." That's all he said. I had learned at this company not to ask questions and said, "Thank you. What's on the docket for tonight?"

Now, we could all critique this change in leadership and the transition. We can absolutely question if there was no extra work to do, why the "two twelves" mantra? Or, why the BS?

In that culture, long hours were a bit of pride. Not productivity, but long hours. If you worked 12s, no matter how little work you did, you were a hero.

It wasn't about how much work you did or how many you helped; it was just how many hours showed up on the punch card. And yes, the company paid for overtime.

Why did I put up with this?

I had dropped out of college and didn't have a great skillset. This job paid about double the minimum wage, mostly due to the normal 30 hours of weekly overtime. I felt lucky to have this job and it was more about survival than thriving.

Thankfully, my career has progressed considerably since this time. But, for a few years, many things like the "two 12s" occurred for seemingly no reason. Some people there worked 40 years in those conditions and considered themselves lucky to have their jobs. Most had a weary look in their eyes, rarely smiled, and were considerably overweight. Other than our work, we didn't talk about much else. Other than the annual company picnic, we didn't hang out outside of work either.

Like many of you who can reflect on difficult jobs you have had, I can remember how I felt - frightened, stuck, and angry. I kept the anger bottled up inside because it would probably only result in my being fired. Even early in my career, I knew there was a better way to run a productive organization, a different way to create high performing teams, and another approach to leadership other than domination.

CHAPTER 6

Death By Meeting

Years ago, I worked at a high-tech company in Silicon Valley that had large all-employee events every few months. They went to great lengths to get a few thousand of us in one place, have catering, swag and the like. Usually, there were one or two C-level speakers who would read us their slides. The expectation was that we would clap for them and cheer them on, even if the slides were awful or we didn't agree.

Many extroverts and some executives would tout this approach as amazing. But did it move the dial? Did we serve our customers better? Were we more efficient? Did we produce more? Were we more innovative? Wait, were any of these results even roughly tracked?

You guessed it, in a word - no. Most of the engineering-based organizations were introverts; most had very strong tech skills and were used to consuming massive amounts of information digitally. Most were used to acting quickly.

One day, I did something unpopular at the time - I put a price tag on those meetings.

Now, social gatherings at work that build camaraderie and serve all who are there (not just the c-levels presenting) can have great value. There are many soft gains to be had by socializing. I'd give bonus points to these meetings if there's a way for participation and two-way communication and if speakers/leaders aren't the highest-paid people in the room. However, many of you may be nodding that you have experienced large meetings that aren't that effective.

Aside from getting over it, do the rough math in your head - at least for yourself - about what this meeting costs financially. You may want to keep this to yourself. This can be a great validation for feelings you may have that this meeting is not useful or even wasteful. Here goes an example:

- 100 Junior Engineers @ $x/hour for 3 hours
- 300 Mid-Level Engineers @ $x/hour for 3 hours
- 50 Senior Engineers @ x/hour for 3 hours
- 25 Managers @ x/hour for 3 hours
- 25 Sales Execs @ x/hour for 3 hours
- 25 Marketing Staff @ x/hour for 3 hours
- 10 VPs @ x/hour for 3 hours
- 5 Execs @ x/hour for 3 hours
- 300 Misc Staff @ x/hour for 3 hours
- Catering for everyone at $15/person
- Room rental for 3 hours (if applicable)
- Misc (travel, parking, security, etc.)
- With meeting I'm referring to here, the grand total was $83,500.

So, did this $83k meeting produce a positive ROI? Such a thing could be measured by employee feedback, customer feedback, financial changes, or other measures that make sense to an organization. And to be fair, soft changes can be harder to measure.

Spoiler alert – they weren't rating in any way and to suggest any of this diligence was a trip to the principal's office (or similar).

One simple way to assess if this meeting is useful is just to look yourself in the mirror. Imagine you are talking to one of your customers who is struggling financially. Then say, "I was a good steward of your money today. Thank you." If that feels awful, gross and dishonest - then that meeting was probably not super useful to your customers. You can do the same exercise for employees if you are a manager - "I made great use of your precious time today."

Again, not every meeting can be monetized like this. And maybe they should be, to at least shape the number of meetings and outcomes that can occur.

Yes, today, many of these meetings are held online, such as on Zoom and Microsoft Teams, so there's no catering, room rental, or other in-person expenses. There's still an investment in staff time, even if they are multi-tasking or chatting with others about whatever the PowerPoints say. It's also likely that the outcomes of these meetings are not measured like other work products.

In the case of my previous company mentioned the costs of those meetings totaled over $1M per year. The leadership was set on having these meetings because of tradition. If they were being honest, the meetings were for the dopamine rush of people clapping for them in a large setting. There was an unspoken message that we are the executives, and you need to be a team player on this. This is very much their call as an executive, and that role can be challenging. If the ideas employees share to make changes are seen as noise or in the way of progress, it can make sense they would be ignored. However, nobody should be surprised if these meetings didn't have outcomes that would move the company forward.

That company collapsed due to high overhead, being disrupted by other technologies, and missing the mark on some of their directions. They weren't alone, as this was common in the late 1990s for tech companies. While Monday morning quarterbacking isn't fair, I still wonder if a few little tweaks to measurement, efficiencies and feedback would have occurred, would that company still exist today?

So, aside from my personal experience with this one organization, what do the many BS things corporations result in? What are the costs and people impact on a larger scale, and what are the trends?

As it turns out, corporate BS issues are more significant than just the buzz of stories at happy hour. Corporate BS has major financial impacts and wastes the potential of their workforce. Here are three findings about these impacts:

- Inefficiencies cost many organizations as much as 20 to 30 percent of their revenue each year." says publishing giant Wiley (10). If true, it amounts to $8.2T of waste a year for the USA alone. To put that into perspective, that's larger than the GDP (all the outputs) of Germany and Japan combined. This is also 10 times the size of Amazon's annual revenue in 2022.
- In this modern day of automation and AI, it's stunning to learn that nearly half of employees are still manually copying and pasting data - or hand entering it. According to an IDC

White Paper (11), "56% of information workers often have to print out a document and then scan it."

- The same study above found those executives shared their staff, on average "spends more than one-third (36%) of their time on administrative tasks — and less than two thirds (64%) on their core job function."

SECTION TWO

Is it time to leave?

If it is that time, know the best steps to take to benefit you long-term.

CHAPTER 7

Time To Say Goodbye

"Take this job and shove it. I ain't working here no more."

—Johny Paycheck

Why not just leave? Why not just start your own company or side hustle?

If meetings are killing you, and maybe you have your own "two twelves" experience going on, why not just walk away from your job?

Okay, there are days (weeks?) when we might fantasize about giving our current job the middle finger. In the movie we create in our minds, we might have some dramatic scene where we tell off our bosses and then go to another job. In that new job, everything is easy; we are paid double, and we live happily ever after.

And there are some with stories of doing just that (or close to it). While it may be a great story, and the movie we create about it in our heads can get us excited, this might not be the first or best course of action.

Now, a lot of attention in business books is given to "live your passion" and to work the job of your dreams. Many times in my career (especially early on), I've lived that mantra. Luckily, that put me in the lucrative field of computer science and IT, but not everyone has the same geeky passions.

In his amazing book, "So Good They Can't Ignore You," Cal Newport makes an interesting comparison of this Passion Mindset and what he calls the Craftsman Mindset. "Whereas the craftsman mindset focuses on what you can offer the world, the passion mindset focuses instead on what the world can offer you."

Now, that's a big shift in thinking, and it can take some time to get this shift. Nobody suggests that you stay in an oppressive job or that you should shut down your dreams. However, you have a path of experiences and education behind your current role. With that foundation, you have an opportunity to build on this and take it further. Sometimes, we can get emotional and lose sight of that, and it can have long-term consequences for our careers.

Without naming specifics here, I've had cases in my career where hot emotions lead to poor long-term decision outcomes. I was a well-regarded Tech Director for a company growing like crazy. My team respected me, and we accomplished a lot. I had a reputation for delivering much faster and higher quality than was expected. And yes, I was getting an ego about it. I was convinced that I was smarter than my boss… and the company that acquired us. This belief was dangerous.

While I'm not proud of it, I let my pride and emotions get the best of me, and my timing and ego lead to some career-limiting positions. I was also going through turmoil in my personal life, so my short fuse was even shorter than normal. In short order, I went from making 6 figures (with a 6-figure bonus) to unemployment. When I finally found a job, months later, it was a 50% cut in pay. It took nearly 10 years for me to get back to the same pay levels and role. Trust me, while I learned many lessons from this, it's not a path I recommend.

There's a time and place for passion, and "always on" is not a great mode for your career.

Given my experience and the fact that you are probably experiencing massive BS in your work life if you are reading this book, let me first offer an approach to assess if you want to leave.

Then, we'll go through a tool to decide the timing and a checklist of things to do to make sure you are doing the best for yourself in the long term as well as the short term.

Are you ready to leave?

Transitioning away from a job, even one you might hate, has serious consequences. In the heat of upset, you might not realize all of these. It's worth it to yourself to step back and look at a few things. Find 30 minutes in your week and take notes as you reflect and answer these questions. The good news is that there are only right answers here - yours!

1. Why are you leaving?

Be honest with yourself here. Drop the F-bomb if you have to. Are you leaving because your boss pisses you off? What specifically do they do (or not do)? Are there co-workers that are annoying? What makes them annoying?

Get very specific here. If you have specific events, that's useful. It is also okay if some of the reasons seem "petty" when you write them down. Do your best not to judge yourself here.

2. What does the next step up look like at your current job?

This might take some imagination and be hard if you are overwhelmed with frustration. Do your best to let that go for a moment.

Is there anyone at your company you admire or a role that you admire? For a different role, this can even be a step (or two) up or a lateral move. If there is, what about those roles do you admire?

If there isn't a role you admire, could you imagine one? Is there a job that needs to be done that nobody is doing, or nobody is doing well?

3. Where do you want to go?

On this one, don't go too deep. We aren't looking for full self-realization and meditating for three years on a mountaintop. Well, I suppose you could choose that but that's a different book.

Think for a bit of where you want to go with your career. Is there a specific title you'd like in five years? Is there a type of work you'd like to be doing? Is there a specific company or field that excites you?

Think briefly about the 2-3 steps you would need to take - at this company or another - to get there. As one of my colleagues likes to ask people, "What's your next-next job?" – what job would you want after your next one?

4. If you are feeling stuck here and can't see forward.

Note that, too. You can create a placeholder until the vision becomes clear. One idea that can work here is to imagine just one notch up the corporate ladder. Yes, that might feel trite, and the exercise of thinking of where you want to go is an important muscle to build up. You can always think of what a director role (if you are a manager) would look like for you. What do you need for that?

And, even if you are all that and a bag of chips, still imagine a few things you would need to do or experiences to be even more valuable to an employer.

5. Money money money...

Do you have 3-6 months of funds set aside? This would be liquid money, and ideally not your 401k.

Even if you have an immediate job offer, or think you do, do you have the means to cover yourself for up to 3-6 months?

You can be creative here, too - could you live with friends or family for a time, sell your car, or take other actions to stretch out your savings?

If you don't have this, it's not a hard "no" to leaving, but an important consideration. This also gives you some action items to focus on. Can you sell something or make do with less for a few months to get there?

This is not to squelch your dreams but to make sure you have a solid foundation and don't fall into another trap because you are so pissed off you can't think right now.

6. The Next Job

Okay, maybe you have a new job lined up or soon to be lined up. The grass may seem greener. It may be at first. And, in time, some of the same patterns will probably come up.

Be careful at seeing lots of job opportunities elsewhere as your primary reason for leaving. While there may be many listings, it doesn't mean you will land any of them. Sorry to be harsh here, but companies can create listings they have no intention of filling with external talent. Many organizations have policies or regulations that force them to post all positions, whether they are available or not. Sometimes, these jobs are actually internal promotions that would be nearly impossible for an outside person to achieve.

If you don't already have contact with the new potential employer, you'll want to get one. Applying to a listing has a slim chance of hiring. Do your best to find a connection on LinkedIn and see if you can get an informational interview for 15 minutes.

What's interesting here, and easy to forget when applying, is that studies show that (7) "70% of jobs are never published publicly. These jobs are either posted internally or are created specifically for candidates that recruiters meet through networking."

While it can seem hard to network and easy to just click and type, the results are with the "hard" stuff here – a little networking.

7. Life-Work Balance

Your health - physical and mental - is precious. While it's likely there are stressors that are overwhelming in your current job, could you learn the skills to overcome them? Is that even a possibility? If it's not, that might be the clearest sign it's time to leave.

However, also consider if that stressor might show up in the next job. While you might get a break from leaving this one, it could be a good time to build up some coping skills. We can help with that with some skill ideas (later in this book). You may also want to consider other resources here to boost yourself at work.

Please consider what it would be like without whatever work toxins you have now. How would you sleep, eat, feel? Is that exceptionally better or just a meh?

8. Who can you talk to?

"Though you may not waaant me to... I'm still gonna taaalk to you."

- Jimmy Fallon on the mythical Barry Gibb talk show

Most of us have friends and family we commiserate with on our work bullshit. Do you have someone *outside* of this circle you could chat with? This could be a mentor at a different company, a college professor, a pastor, or someone you admire - whatever works for you.

It's worth at least 30 minutes chatting with that person to get their perspective. They may agree with you, and they may give you new ideas. When we are in these situations, it is hard to see all our options. Hearing someone out and having them hear us out can help us make the best choices.

Yes, this list of seven items requires some work, and it's harder than just cursing out your current boss for being a tool. While name-calling and describing the current place (and/or boss) with your favorite expletives might help with venting - it's not likely moving you forward.

This short reflection is worth it - as are you - in shaping your decisions.

Exit Stage Left - Your Checklist

"So, you got to let me know.
Should I stay or should I go?"

— **The Clash**

Okay, if you have done the work and made the decision to go, this will help you make this decision the most powerful it can be for you. You may need to bite your tongue and do a few things that feel unnatural at first. That's okay. Remember, you are going for a long-term gain for yourself here.

Oh, and if you aren't sure yet, skip this section and know it is here for you later. I'm not advocating that this is your only option, or that you need to act right this second. Lots of you might be thinking of ways to deal with the BS or escape it in your current company. You are still a badass if you do this, too. There's lots of tools (the good kind) later in the book for you.

What To Expect If You Are Expecting

While the subtitle of this section is intended to put a smile on your face, the stress of a new job and routine is significant. Maybe it's different from bringing a new precious life into the world, but it's probably just behind that. Remember that most of our time from our 20s to our 60s is spent with co-workers. Whoa. So, because of all these emotions, it is smart to create a checklist to make sure you don't have a blind spot to something important long term.

Before you give notice:

1. Have a secure offer (signed paperwork) with a start date. While it's rare, even this isn't a sure thing. I have several friends that have been burned with signed offers disappearing. Not trying to scare you here, but be aware. This is why it's also important to have that savings of 3-6 months if you can.

2. Obtain recommendations from co-workers and leaders. If you don't think your direct leader will give you a good review, ask other leaders who you think will. Also, you can ask co-workers, too. To help with any suspicions, you can say you just read it's good to have these on your LinkedIn and wanted to add some. You can offer to write them a good review if you are motivated to do so.

3. Create a timeline for yourself. Give yourself a few days between jobs. Let go of the last one before focusing on your new role. You may consider some self-care like a massage, hike in nature, or something that helps you reset. If you cannot do this, consider working in some self-care over the first two weeks of your role.

4. Practice being thankful and gracious. While it's tempting to drop swear bombs and complain, hoping that "you'll get them," this rarely works out. However, if you leave your job in a gracious and classy way, that will be remembered. You may be surprised and work with some of these people again. Again, while it is so tempting to be "right" and "show them," you will only hurt yourself. You can privately vent this anger and upset. Doing something physical can help your body

release this - heavy weights, a big run, squats and pushups until you can't, and even screaming into your hand.

5. Prepare how and when you give notice. If at all possible, do it live. If you work remotely, this means over the phone. If you cannot do this, corporate email is the next best bet. When you prepare your words, also prepare not to say too much. You don't have to answer questions and can say, "That's really all I'm prepared to say now, thank you." You can also respond with something like, "I can totally appreciate how this is a shock. I'm happy to help with transition planning and any knowledge transfer over the next two weeks. Maybe we should touch base in a day as this news is new?" Also be prepared that your current leader might not say much at all. Don't take this personally.

After you give notice:

1. Ask your leader if it's okay to tell people about this decision or if they want to do it. While it's tempting just to tell everyone, realize that many people still need to work at this place. You don't need to make it ugly for them, and honestly that doesn't serve you. Soon enough, they will all know. Your leader may need to get approval for a backfill or other activities and need a day or two to make that happen.

2. Separate your work talk from your happy hour talk. Work and personal lives have grayed for all of us. However, what you might say with a friend at happy hour should differ from what you say at work. Practice being the new professional at your new job.

3. While it's easy to feel checked out now, stay engaged as best you can. This time is similar to the days before a big vacation, where you have to work extra preparing things so you can later relax. All the logistics of a trip - packing, confirming reservations, dealing with travel issues - can make you need that vacation even more, right? Realizing that you are leaving this job may also create a sense of loss for co-workers, even if they don't directly express that. Think of a time when someone you loved working with left - that bright light not being around can bum people out.

4. Resist recruiting others. There will be many wanting to know where you are going, what you are doing, and if they are hiring. These are normal human questions. I suggest you have those conversations on personal channels - not at work or on work systems. You can also say something like, "Hey, reach out in two weeks, and let's talk." This can separate the gossip stuff from people interested in taking action.

5. Plan your exit interview. While not every organization does this, the exit interview can be a tempting time to vent. We can play a movie in our heads about getting justice and finally telling it like it is. It's tempting, and you can do this. However, think about the likely outcomes. Often, this activity is a checkbox for HR to have in case there's a lawsuit later. Sure, they may care a little, but any actions taken are likely small. You can leave an amazing impression on this HR person, who will remember that. If there are legal issues at play, this is also not the place for that. You'll want to follow the corporate procedures to report these and potentially engage your own lawyer. But the exit interview isn't the

place for this. If you are asked questions that are too uncomfortable for you, just say, "I'm sorry, I'm just not comfortable answering that question. Can I help with something else?"

6. Connect and empathize. Many will contact you and share they are sad to see you go but happy for you. Take a few seconds to acknowledge that this event is hard for them. If you want bonus points, validate their feelings. This costs you nothing and gains you a ton. You may have these contacts for a long time and need them when you least expect it.

7. Celebrate outside of work. With friends, family, or even by yourself, celebrate your choice. You've made a hard decision and taken big actions. Oh, and if the "oh, my gosh, what am I doing" message starts playing, just thank it for being concerned. If the new job doesn't work out, you can make another decision later. And, you don't know if the new job will work out or not.

SECTION THREE

Are Side Hustles for you?

Explore what may, and may not, make sense for you.

CHAPTER 8

Side Hustles

On Facebook, YouTube, Instagram, Twitter, TikTok, and everywhere else, there are some videos or messages playing about how you can start a side hustle and leave your daily job.

Usually, these messages push a free webinar and then a low-end book or course. They later want to schedule a call with you and then pitch an expensive program. They will also show you examples of those who made millions in their first year.

Social media has amazing data and tools for advertisers that help them target people. While these messages could seem like they happened or you found them, it's more likely that they found you based on your online behavior. Also, while these are exciting opportunities, do the math. The results are often for less than 3% of those in the program. You may be the exceptional one in this program, and you may not be.

Let me first be clear: I'm not against a side hustle. Side hustles can be an interesting way to test out different career options and can even give relief to you financially. So, on the positive side of side hustles, let me walk you through one that worked well for me. Later, I'll walk you through one that didn't.

Wax On Wax Off

About a decade ago, while I had a stable job, I was struggling financially. Making ends meet every month was tough. Even with a great job, supporting two kids and cleaning up some mess from the past was challenging. I had two rental properties. Before you think I was a mogul, I had to move out of some tough situations, and it was go upside down on the houses or rent them and try to save my credit score. Both rentals were slightly cash-negative, which was stressful. I could also not sell them as the housing market was at a low. Adding to the fun, I also had a renter who stopped paying, and so I was going through six months of the eviction process with them. My mindset was overwhelmed, and I had somewhat decided that I was already too busy. I did not consider how I could do anything more than find a higher-paying job. Sound familiar?

To understand the options to help with my financial mess and over-commitments, I read many books by people like Dave Ramsey and Suze Orman. Some of what they wrote woke me up to what I was doing that trashed my financial future. I inspected my "looking good" needs – especially my need to drive a nice car. For years, I attached a lot of status to having a nice car - be it an Audi, BMW or Mercedes. I looked at what the nicest car I could afford from a monthly payment perspective. And because of my pride here, I would often change out cars every two years and lose money every time.

The other big awakening for me was realizing that, even though I was busy, I could do a side job. I remember Dave Ramsey suggesting in his books to deliver pizzas as a side job. After reflecting, I thought about what I could do with something I already knew that wouldn't be a conflict of interest to my current job. While it might seem like "none of their business," some employers have written and unwritten rules about conflicts of interest. Usually, you need to declare any other engagement outside of work and be clear that you aren't using that employer to promote your side gig.

Okay, back to our story. So, I realized that I had been detailing cars - my own and my friends - since I was nine years old. To refresh my skills, I watched a lot of free videos on YouTube. I also found a third-party group that certifies detailers and began that process. I found reasonable insurance coverage, so I was covered just in case, and then I started things out. My goal at first was to get visual evidence I was a good detailer. To do this, I asked a few friends with Porsches and other nice cars if they wanted a free detail. Well, it wasn't totally free. The payment that they would give me would be photos and reviews. It was the middle of winter when I started, and not ideal for mobile detailing, but I did it anyway. In short order, I had detailed images of Porsches, Mercedes, and other nice cars, along with reviews. This made it a lot easier for a customer to feel safe when choosing me.

Soon after this, I engaged with the local Cars and Coffee community and let them know I was detailing. I was doing this for my kid's college funds, which gave me a compelling story and an edge over some other detailers. Having references and images – from my free details - helped, too. Along with a handful of paying clients, I landed a large car collector who needed weekly service. While he took a risk with me, he also got a great price, and I added to my client photos a number of exotic cars, which always get attention.

Was I exhausted? Yes, at times, I was. However, using my energy to do something about my mess instead of just sitting in it gave me more energy. This side hustle was also a great workout. Even better, unlike my day job, it had instant gratification and payment that day. No long, drawn-out decision-making, committees, or months to see results. My work was done that day, paid that day, with a dramatic before and after. It was gratifying to see the dramatic before and after results. Detailing at the time also paid between $40-100/hour, much better than delivering pizzas. While there were some equipment and material costs, they weren't huge, and vendors gave me a discount as a business owner. Because I already had some expertise here, I didn't need to invest in any online program. My instincts and experience were good enough.

So, what worked well in this side hustle example?

- **Thinking out of the box** - Asking myself what I may already know and how I could do it moved the dial and produced results. Trying the same things that didn't work again and again (higher paying job, stressing out, etc.) produced no results.

- **Rising above** - Asking myself, "How could I" instead of lamenting the mess I was in produced results. To get to this honestly took me a few months. I thought I didn't have enough energy. I convinced myself that I didn't have enough energy.

- **Working Out of It** - While I could have considered bankruptcy or other approaches, working out of this mess, albeit challenging, set me up for success long-term. It was also cathartic and gave me a lot of pride.

- **Using What I Know** - Instead of some new scheme to make money, I leveraged a knowledge set I already had and could build on. And while I loved cars, the hard work of detailing wasn't entirely a passion.
- **Testing It Out** - Doing a few free details helped with reviews and proof of results for other clients. However, it also validated that I could do this, would enjoy doing it enough to keep going, and helped to iron out some mistakes before serving paying clients.
- **Physical and Local** - While there are thousands of digital and global side hustles, there's something about building one locally. You will build stronger relationships. It's easier to test things out, and it's honestly less costly. You don't need paid ads.

As things spun up, there were some good things and bad things about this side hustle. It got to where I needed a shop (physical location) to scale but wasn't ready to do that. I had one employee who worked his tail off. However, the revenues weren't there for me to do more than break even with that employee. I made money on the detail work I did myself. Over a year, the profit from the work I did myself was around $27k. I also enjoyed several tax write-offs. After doing this for about four years, I spun it down. However, I still have a handful of clients who won't take no for an answer and pay me for high-end details. I'm honored to serve them.

Okay, as good as this detailing side hustle was for me, I have dozens of "doom" stories here. Yes, I have done "those" webinars, bought their buy-ups, enrolled in some high-end programs and believed I would make "6 figures". Usually, I lost money or at best, broke even. I saw most of my colleagues in these programs do much worse. Only 2% of the people enjoyed the results claimed by the program. Ouch.

Beware of The Seductive Sales Cycles

As much as my detail side hustle was primarily a success (nothing is perfect), I've made a lot of mistakes in approaching other side hustles. And if I can help anyone else avoid these nightmares, I would love to!

As some background, once, I went deep into learning about social media ads - Facebook, Instagram, YouTube and TikTok. I also went deep into email marketing and achieved certification from one of the experts and OGs in that space. For a few years, I did this as a side hustle for a few small businesses.

Please understand - it's relatively easy to target those looking for a side hustle. The pain points of people in this space are well known. It's also straightforward to create videos, images and messages that interrupt your social media feed. While you are enjoying that social media dopamine rush, these ads can get you to pay for programs almost before you know you have.

Many of these programs are well-intentioned and seek to serve their audiences. However, there are many that are exceptional at getting your money and poor at delivering value. Often, these programs may blame you for not acting (even when you are), or that you aren't following their program perfectly. Beware of these. They are great at selling you but poor at delivering value.

Again, while there are good actors here, there are also entire industries that prey on people making impulsive decisions. Their goal is to have people buy their high-ticket programs. Some justify this approach as their program being so great, and they must resort to manipulation to get people unstuck and into their programs. While maybe there's some truth to that, also look at the real success rates of their programs. You will probably see a few dozen testimonials that seem compelling as part of their ad sequences. However, stop, take a second and do the math here. If they claim, for example, to have served 1000 people and they have 12 testimonials, that means that only 1.2% of their students will share their success. Also, reach out to those 12 people (in this example). You can find them on FB, LinkedIn or other places. See if they will sing the praises of the program in a private message or if it's something else. Remember, you are making an investment in your precious money and precious time here - make sure you are informed.

Do your best not to buy the program based on some false scarcity. Sellers of programs will have countdown sequences or "special deals" on webinars to boost conversion rates. It's easy to click buy on these or feel like you'll miss out if you don't. Trust me, I've done it more than once. I've also helped set up many of these sequences for others. Without them, the conversion rates are about half, which is why you still see them in use – they work for the seller.

Please also understand there will be people "finding you" to push these ads and email sequences. There's a massive amount of tech, behavioral science and marketing in play to make the sellers successful. However, making you successful can often be an afterthought - and that's what *you* want.

If you get sucked in and it doesn't work, forgive yourself and move on. You can write off the business expenses of the program if you form an LLC. Your time is precious. Count this as a learning activity, yourself being smarter, and keep moving forward.

If you want to avoid being the 98% that fail in these side hustles, here's a framework to evaluate if a specific side hustle is the right thing for you. While the webinars and "buy now" special offers are compelling, stop and take this quick test to set yourself up for success.

Side Hustle Assessment

Please use this as a guideline, and not the end-all, be-all for your journey into side hustles. As always, be honest with yourself because you deserve that!

Evaluate how you rate this side hustle opportunity for you after answering these questions.

1. How many years of experience do you have in this side hustle?

    a) None really - 0 points

    b) Under a Year - 3 Points

    c) 1-5 Years - 5 points

    d) 5-10 Years - 7 points

    e) 10+ Years - 10 points

2. Have you made money doing something like this side hustle before?

    a) No - 0 points

    b) No, but did some volunteer work using this skill - 5 points.

c) Yes - 8 points

3. Does this side hustle come within 25% of your current hourly wage? You can estimate your hourly wage by taking your salary and dividing it by 2112 (12 months * 22 working days a month * 8 hours a workday). So, for example, $100k would be $47.34/hour. You would want your side hustle to be at least $35 and, ideally, a lot closer to $50/hour.

   a) Yes, it's within 25% of my current hourly rate - 10 points.
   b) No, I would make less than this - 5 points
   c) I have no clue or don't want to do math - 0 points.

4. How many hours per weekday and weekend can you dedicate to your side hustle?

   a. hour a week - 1 point
   b) 1-5 hours a week - 3 points
   c) 5-10 hours a week - 5 points
   d) 10-20 hours a week - 8 points
   e) 20+ hours a week - 10 points

5. How much start-up money do you have set aside for your side hustle?

   a) $0-$1000 - 7 points
   b) $1000-$5000 - 8 points
   c) $5000+ - 9 points

6. Are you responding to a new program or social media ad for their course or program that is a new space for you?

    a) Yes - 0 points

    b) No - 8 points

7. Do you know anyone in this space you can talk to?

    a) Yes - 8 points

    b) No - 0 points

8. Could you see yourself doing this side hustle full-time?

    a) Yes - 8 points

    b) No - 0 points

9. Will this side hustle create any conflict of interest - real or perceived - with your current job?

    a) Yes, it might - 0 points.

    b) No, it shouldn't - 10 points.

10. Imagine yourself 5 years from now; where will this side hustle fit in your life?

    a) It would still be a side hustle - 7 points

    b) It could be my main job - 7 points

    c) It would no longer be a side hustle - 5 points

    d) I have no idea and don't want to think about it - 0 points.

Scoring Your Results

Crank up your honesty, even if you don't love the answers right now. You may improve and act on some of these to get the goals you want. Or you may re-assess and find a different side hustle (or no hustle at all right now).

70-100 Points - This may be a great side hustle to check out. Try your idea out with sample customers (like the car detail example) to make sure you love it and that your customers love and see value in what you do.

50-70 Points – Think about re-assessing this side hustle. Tweak its components or find another side hustle that's a better fit.

Under 50 Points - Either the timing isn't right for this, or it's likely the wrong side hustle. Now, these words might be a rallying cry - "I'll show you!" If that's the case, please consider time-boxing your side hustle efforts and check in at 30, 60 and 90 days in to see if you still love it. If you don't, you don't need to be stuck and can either pivot to something else or take a break. Most successful entrepreneurs tried a lot of things and refined a ton before they hit their sweet spot.

SECTION FOUR

What matters most?

Understand your unique guiding principles and what matters most to you.

SECTION FOUR

What matters most

CHAPTER 9

Your Goals and Why

"Everyone has a plan until they get punched in the face."

— *Mike Tyson*

Okay, so something about your current work environment had you pick up this book. Some BS is going on that you want to avoid, overcome, or leave, right?

Yep, I get it. I've been there many times during my career. I have ping-ponged between roles because I was not yet grounded in my why. I let the circumstances dictate my outcomes instead of heading towards something larger.

Early in our careers, going from job to job more often is common. A recent Gallup report (13) found that 1 in 5 millennials have changed jobs in the last 12 months - "which is more than three times the number of non-millennials who report the same." While it might be easy to label a generation, there's an age in career function that's applied here as well. When GenX-ials were in their early 20s, they changed jobs at a similar pace because there was the opportunity to do so. According to a Fortune article (19) "BLS figures, older millennials—those born between 1980 and 1984—had held an average of seven jobs by age 28." So, did the Baby Boomers also do this when they were young? Yes, they bopped around as well. This is more about age in career and less about generational differences.

However, later in our careers, this pace of change, according to BLS statistics, slows. This is likely due to career progression, priorities in life, and the number of opportunities. This is consistent, no matter what generation a person was born into.

In the tech community especially, there are many jobs, more work than people, and high pay available. This isn't available in every field, but you can more easily see the pattern in tech.

During the boom cycles of the dotcom world in the late 1990s, it was common for some tech workers to spend only 9 months at a job. Often, they would be paid in stock equity, and when the company went public, they cashed out and went on to the next company.

Often, in this boom-and-bust cycle, their chosen employer of the day might have gone under. Knowing that many jobs were available and the pay was high, many in their 20s took this risk.

There is a bit of brain science at play here. While our younger selves can think that they are invincible and know everything, their brains are still growing and maturing. According to several sources, including the National Institutes of Health [20] "The development and maturation of the prefrontal cortex occurs primarily during adolescence and is fully accomplished at the age of 25 years."

This is somewhat similar to those who figure out their college major after trying a few classes. Back in the dark ages, when I went to school, I thought I wanted to be a pre-veterinary major. That required a number of classes that were tricky for me, including advanced botany. Memorizing plant names was not my jam. After those courses and hanging out with people with that major, I realized that I didn't really want to do this. While it sounds trite, my initial interest in veterinary medicine was shaped by the great experiences I had at the San Diego Wild Animal Park. I went there often, and once, I splurged on a Jeep tour, where I got to feed giraffes and rhinos by hand. It was an amazing experience and I glamorized this could be my job and world. Queue the theme music!

However, I didn't have the chops or a strong enough why to do the work for that major. Also, the lifestyle it would involve - relatively low pay and deployed to places all over the world - didn't match what I really wanted. While I didn't do the "why" work then to re-adjust, I did fall back on something easy for me - Computer Science. The coursework, lifestyle, and income matched what I wanted to do, and I had both the skill and interest to make this happen. Until then, my tech interests were just something fun for me and a hobby. However, given some energy, focus, and community, that hobby soared into a lucrative career.

While it's important to have some sort of why and goals to shape long-term outcomes, please know that some ping-ponging around is normal. Just don't let it be your lifelong pattern, going from one job to the next every few months. Decades of that will be exhausting.

To help, the approach we will go through here in a moment might differ from what you are used to. While it's frankly weird, we often actually celebrate how bad things are. Our friends and family may join in on this negative agreement. This pattern is strong in middle school and high school - you can get a lot of attention when talking about something that "sucks". It is easy to make connections around this negative talk. This middle school talk often continues into adulthood.

"'"bunchafuckinbullshit" - Dana Carvey, joking about his teenage son's reaction to things.

In a stand-up routine, Dana Carvey depicts this phrase in an absolutely hilarious manner, talking about his teenage son. When Carvey asks him to do something he doesn't like, his response can be to slump his shoulders down, sulk away and swear under his breath. Carvey even imitates his walk.

While it's easy to laugh at this, we often do this when talking about work issues. While we might not literally sulk away and swear under our breath, we can feel like things are being done to us and aren't fair. Sometimes that is accurate, and sometimes, we are being a drama king/queen because we aren't anchored.

So, knowing we all have some drama and that we probably don't want to ping-pong our whole career, we should just make goals, checklists and grind it out, right?

Well, maybe. But that has some issues, too.

> "Many problems can't be solved forward."
>
> — *Charlie Munger*

If it were as easy as setting goals, like a New Year's resolution, we would all be living the life of our dreams already, right? The data on that is staggering. Maybe you have made a New Year's resolution and did it for a bit, but then it fell apart. It's easy then to fall into a shame cycle here where you start to beat up on yourself, feel worse, and spiral into more unhealthy actions. Recent Forbes research (16) showed that "the average resolution lasts just 3.74 months". Other studies (17) show that only 9% succeed in keeping their New Year's resolutions. In our data and insight-heavy world, there's even a known day for most New Year's resolutions to end - it's January 19, which is known as "quitters day" (18).

Okay, so if we (as a race) cannot keep our goals for long, can ping pong between jobs, and can be drama kings (and queens) swearing about our circumstances, what should we consider instead?

Focus instead on your why and your principles.

Who we are and who we want to be are a lot stronger than the events, goals, successes, and failures that come and go throughout our lives. The more we can build these up and keep them as a focus, the less likely we are to get sucked into work and life drama.

There are many ways to connect with your why. There are thousands of books, programs, and gurus on this subject. It's also very easy to get lost in "finding yourself" as a lifelong journey.

For this book and for right now, let's keep it simple. Here's an easy exercise to help you reflect, find your why and develop principles. What's great about this and everything in life is that you can always change and refine things later. So, if you find yourself in something like "I'm not sure." or "sorta" or "it's close but not quite right" - that's okay. Pick the thing (more on that shortly) and keep going. You can tweak it later. Staying on the sidelines is a decision that will not lead to your happiness and will keep you stuck. So, even if it's awkward or not quite right, it's way better to be on the field with that than watching your life pass by.

> *"If you choose not to decide, you still have made a choice."*
>
> *— Rush, Freewill*

Your Why Exercise

It is tricky to find out our why. Many spend a lifetime "finding themselves" in hopes of some clarity or divine wisdom. While those can be noble pursuits, let's get you some immediacy here instead so you can keep going.

Imagine yourself at 85, talking to elementary school kids. Or, if it's easier, imagine writing a letter to yourself from 85 to yourself today.

In that talk or in that letter, include:

- What was important about your life?
- What advice would you give this younger generation? What should they worry (or not worry) about?
- What do you wish you did more of and less of?
- What were those times that you made difficult choices like? What resulted from those choices?
- What are the things you are most proud of?
- What do you wish you spent less time on?

Take somewhere between 20 minutes to an hour. You are worth it this time. Be thoughtful as you craft your talking points or write your letter. On your paper, you have described what matters to you most and who you are (and seek to be more of). You are looking for a career that aligns with this as much as is reasonably possible. Seal this letter and put it somewhere safe, and then put a calendar reminder to read it a year from now.

CHAPTER 10

Who Do You Want To Be

> *"Who do you want to be today?*
> *Who do you want to be?*
> *Who do you want to be today?*
> *Do you want to be just like someone on TV?"*
> **-Oingo Boingo, Who Do You Want to Be**

There are many great approaches to getting to our why. Some gurus have year-long programs that will help people get great epiphanies. I will not go to those depths in the next few pages because we aren't that good (or that guru'd). But I will help you come up with your directional whys.

I will add a few non-career items here, too. Because you bring your "you" to the workplace anyway, and things outside of work affect your work results. Go figure.

Message to You Rudy

> *"Stop your messing around, Better think of your future."*
> **-The Specials, Message to You Rudy**

One great way to get a sense of your why is to think of yourself, say 10-20 years from now. Take a little time to imagine yourself there. If it's not clear, use your imagination to make things up that work for you. Consider what your career may be then, what your family may look like (if you have one of your own), where you may live, what you enjoy doing with your friends, and where you might travel on vacations.

Once you have that image in your mind (you likely need to stop reading for a little bit here for this to work - hint, hint) - think of a letter to write to your younger self now. Pretend that your future self could write a letter to you, and it would magically reach you now. The letter would be full of advice, coaching and ideas. So, what would it say?

To get the most out of this, take fifteen minutes and write that letter to yourself. Yes, this might feel weird at first. That's okay, keep going. It will be weird only for a short time. From your future self's point of view, what would they recommend? Would they suggest courses to take for your career? Would they recommend you stay at your current employer? Would they recommend any specific side hustles?

In addition to the career side of things, what does your future self-recommend for your life? Is there a sport you always wanted to play or an instrument you want to try out? Is there a place you want to travel to or a language you want to learn? Is there a hobby you want to do more of?

What you are doing in this exercise is using your own amazing cerebral cortex. Absent of the "I can't's" and "I don't know how's" that we can tie ourselves up with, we have some incredible and often untapped brain power. These problem-solving, creative, and imaginative parts of our brains are insanely powerful. When we tune into them, they can truly guide us. This usually requires us to step out of our "stuff" and get calm while also getting centered. In this state, we need to listen to our own ideas flow. And, like any muscle, this practice needs exercise to get stronger. You won't do the equivalent of a 500 lb. bench press your first time out. That's okay.

The Trip to the Principles Office

"Eleven hours in the tin pan God, there's got to be another way."

-The Who, Who Are You

As you imagine and write these letters to yourself, also consider what principles might be important to you. Principles here would mean 5-7 guidelines and directions to assess if things are right for you. What's great about principles is that they last the test of time and are the changes that come about in the world. They don't sway massively in our lifetimes. Some we may already be strong in, and others we aspire to be stronger in. It's important here, though, to stay true to yourself - what matters to you. You don't need to impress anyone or feel like you need to please someone. These principles are for you.

To help get your ideation going, here are principles to consider:

- Integrity
- Resilience
- Self-Discipline
- Kindness

- Learning
- Physical Health
- Responsibility
- Humility
- Social Connections
- Care For Environment

You can use versions of these, the same ones, or none - what matters is that you pick 5-7 that are true to you. Yes, you can pick a few less or a few more.

Now, as you make big decisions (and maybe even medium ones), you have a scale against which to measure them. Not every decision will have perfect balance, but the scale gives you a measuring stick that matters to you. For example, let's say you have the opportunity at a new role in your organization. However, other than the money and prestige, you aren't entirely sure about it. You could use your principles to quickly assess this potential. Let's look at some made-up principles:

- Purpose - Does this role align with your need to give back? Does the role itself give you the free time to work with your charities of choice or time within the job to give back in a way meaningful to you?
- Financial Independence - Does this role provide a better path than you are on to invest more and retire early?
- Learning - Will this role let you learn new skills that matter to you? Will the new leadership help you on this path?

- Integrity - Does this new role require you to compromise on any of your beliefs? If it does, is it worth it?
- Care for the Environment- Does this job match your concerns for the environment? Do you have to make any compromises?

Now, these are just made-up principles, and your mileage may vary. However, as you can see, you have a quick checklist to use. I often score my answers from 1-5 and look at the overall score to help make my decision. If the score is low, I may still take the action. However, because of this scoring exercise, I'm walking in very informed and honest to that decision. The intent here is that you have your own measuring stick to guide you through your career.

Over time, you may focus on different principles that matter to you. By using these to help guide career decisions, you'll find more fulfillment and resilience. Many of the day-to-day angst may fall by the wayside - or have different meanings. We'll get to several skills to help with that later.

Please also know if the BS at work is just too much and you have to leave - and that matches your why and principles - that's what you need to do. This isn't about being a martyr and staying and suffering. Life's too short for that!

CHAPTER 11

What Should Your Work Life Look Like?

The title of this chapter gets most people caught up in our ever-expanding stories of why our work is BS. We usually create some "us vs. them" scenario where we are a harmless victim.

If that reflection stings and hits close to home, you aren't alone. It's easy to list issues about work, and even popular to do so. We like to commiserate. However, we (as humans) often will not see what part we have in the situation. Sometimes, we also have something big (to us) that we don't yet have the skills to deal with, so we package it as BS and tell everyone about how bad it is.

That story can get locked into a part of our brain called the RAS (Reticular Activating System). This part of our brain is what I like to call the "heavy repeat" section, playing your personal top 40 hits on high rotation. The messages in your personal RAS repeat up to 40,000 times a day. That's a lot of times hearing "this sucks" and makes it easy to be stuck with that volume of noise.

Why does our RAS hate us so much? Well, it doesn't hate us at all and is trying to do an important, and maybe primitive function - keep you alive. While we rarely have predators like bears chasing us daily, we still have the brain programs running that think they need to protect us. There's a set of rules in these programs to avoid major stressors as a function of survival. Here's where this gets interesting - it doesn't matter there isn't really a bear about to eat us - if our RAS and threat response systems perceive a threat at that bear-eating level, they activate the same things as if we are about to die. Cortisol and adrenaline pump in high volumes, we lose the use of our higher brain functions, and we are often stuck in a fight, flight or freeze scenario. For most of us reading this book, no matter how stressful, we aren't likely to die at work today. However, the brain chemistry present is acting just as if we were. And if the stressors at this level continue, this can take a major toll on our health.

Now, the RAS must also filter out around 40 million pieces of information a second. After this filter, only about 40,000 messages come in the gateway of the RAS into the higher-functioning parts of our brain. There's also no shortcut - everything you smell, touch, see and hear goes through this gateway.

The RAS is so powerful that it can create a "top hits" list and put them on high rotation. Some of these hits include things like "my boss sucks" and "my work sucks" and perhaps "bunchafuckingbullshit". Interestingly, if any information tries to sneak in that goes against these messages, they will be perceived as a threat and filtered out. The new messages may also receive a wave of messages to try to prove the new message "wrong".

To experience this in action, pick something you don't like about your job. Maybe you cannot stand your current boss, or something at work bugs you to no end. After you have that annoyance in mind, try to say to yourself one nice thing about this person or situation. Yes, I know it might be hard to envision, but pick one small thing. Notice the massive amount of resistance to this new positive message. For example, if you name something positive about a boss you can't stand, notice how many messages come up with something like "yeah, but that doesn't matter because she …" or "but he's a tool the rest of the time and …" For most of us, we'll have a whole slew of negative messages for any new positive information. This is because we've conditioned ourselves - unknowingly - to stay with "work sucks" as a top hit.

The other weird thing we can do as humans is get stuck in being "right" about something. Even if being right creates a massive amount of pain in our lives, we can get stuck there. So, for example, the mythical boss here who is awful begins to make changes and tries to be better. While this may actually be helpful, it is easy to stay stuck in the top hit of "they suck" and not give these changes a chance. We want to be right about them being awful bosses more than we want the results of them changing for the better. Or, in looking at what bothers us, we can want to be right about it being awful, and we should get some hazard pay or reward for enduring it.

Trust me, I've done all these things in my career. There's zero judgment here. I also want you to understand how the natural plumbing in your brain can create these situations - and sometimes make things even worse. When you start to make changes, those top hits will greet you in your threat response system, and your natural need is to be right. If change were easy and simple, you would have done it. Fortunately, you can turn this pattern around. It requires a few simple steps.

First, thank these hits (from your threat response system) for wanting to help you. Let them know you want to try something new that they might even like. You are going to spend your energy asking, "What should your ideal workplace look like?" This may exercise a new line of thoughts for you. Here's an exercise that might help you with this.

Ideal Workplace Exercise

First, we recommend that you take a few moments and get your body calm. Take 5-10 deep breaths, slow things down, and do your best to let go of the current worries. You can reply to them in 10 minutes. With your eyes closed, let go of whatever current work worries you may have. It is helpful to imagine a river flowing by, and these worries floating along down the river. While it might sound silly, you can give them names, colors, and sounds. The more you define them like this, the easier it will be for your brain to package them and put them away for now.

Okay, after a few minutes at the river, take a moment and imagine what your ideal work would be like. You may be confronted with messages like "but I can't have" and "I don't know" - that's okay, thank them and let them go. Get back to your ideal work environment.

What would you be doing?

Create as many stories here as you like. Think if you would work with people, doing analytics on your own, what sort of outputs you would create, and where you may do this ideal work.

What sorts of people do you work with?

If you had the ideal co-workers and boss, what would that be like? Would you be inspired and energized by working with them? What sorts of things would they say to you? How would you interact with them?

What does success look like?

Do you get energized by landing a new deal, or serving a new customer, or being more efficient? Do you enjoy recognition by peers or leaders? Did you produce something creatively or maybe engineer a new solution? Think about what successes look like to you.

How do you feel the Sunday before your work week?

If you loved your job, what would the Sunday before the work week feel like? Instead of dread, would you look forward to things? What would that energy in your body feel like? What would you be excited about?

How do you feel after work?

On your commute home or time after work, how would you feel? Would you have stories about what you accomplished and who you served? Would you have ideas for the next day? Would you have stories for your family and friends? What would they be?

What stories do you tell your loved ones?

Those stories you tell others - the ones that start with something like "you'll never believe what happened" - what will they be? Will they be your accomplishments, or a great thing that happened at work or something you did for someone else?

What's your title?

Zoom out a few years - what is your title? You can make this up and it doesn't have to have a C or VP in it - unless that serves you.

Do you own your company? Can you use creative or funny words to name what you do?

Who is your boss and how are they?

What does your new boss do that's great? How do they encourage you? How do they inspire you?

What's your compensation?

See the new direct deposit in your bank account on payday. What is that new number? What new choices do you make with that number? How do you feel when that arrives?

When can you retire?

While you may work some after retirement, what year of your life do you want to be mostly done with the day-to-day work? Is it earlier than others? What will you do the first day you retire?

What are other details about your work - big or small?

As you are producing this new top hit for your brain, notice any other details. You may create images of the environment or a specific story. Note things big and small in this new environment.

After visualizing this, take a few moments to jot ideas down. Use a diagram, mind map, or drawing. Whatever works for you is okay.

Consider this new map of how you wish things to be. For now, do your best to resist fears about how you may get there or how far away this seems from where you are. What's cool about our brains - since I dissed them earlier in this chapter - is that if you visualize a goal and keep visualizing it - your brain will slowly look for evidence to make this true.

I know this may sound like some woo-woo BS. That would be a different book, and maybe a good one ("Woo Woo BS" and the real deal). However, the same power of creating top hits in our RAS of "works sucks" and "my boss sucks" can also produce new top hits of "this is what I want" and "go find this" and "look for this".

Now, I'm not suggesting merely seek the positive and suck up the crap you are currently experiencing. That's a level of denial and lying to yourself that is toxic. Trust me, I did that for way too long. You are experiencing some BS, and it's okay to acknowledge it. And you don't want that BS to be one of your top hits in your precious life for long.

It will take a little effort to produce your new hits. And you won't always know how to get there. As awkward as this is and strange as it might feel, just having clarity of what things should look like moves you forward.

Now, while there's going to be a lot of things that need to create this "how should it be" world for yourself - and it's easy to go back to "it sucks" - you are worth trying something new out. So, with your notes in hand from this exercise, your new challenge is to consider them every morning for 5 minutes. If you miss a morning, do it later in the day or just catch up the next day. This isn't about shame, it's about progress.

Do this for at least 10 days. As you do it, notice if anything like "I can't" or "I don't know how" come up. You can thank those thoughts (remember RAS is trying to protect you) and put the word yet in back of them - "I can't yet" or "I don't know how yet". While it's tempting to create a path of goals and action items to get to that new world, just getting very crisp on what it looks, sounds, and feels like is more important.

And yes, I know, your current job probably still sucks. While you are playing that top hit, we are creating a new place for you to travel to. This will give you a better target to go to, instead of another job that will also suck - and a much better trajectory. Oh, and if you breezed through this like most people and think that you'll do this later, you probably won't. You are way better off by stopping, doing the exercise soon (if not now), and sticking with it than you are speed reading through the rest of the book. Promise.

"The only limit to the height of your achievements is the reach of your dreams and your willingness to work hard for them." — Michelle Obama

SECTION FIVE

BS Issues and Skills

Enjoy 13 proven skills to overcome BS, along with help identifying BS patterns.

CHAPTER 12

Skills You Can Build

"Just because someone stumbles and loses their way doesn't mean they are lost forever."

— *Jada Pinkett Smith*

Getting through a job progression can be a challenge. Things may have started off relatively easy early in our careers, and as they progressed, we may have found ourselves stuck. Or, early in our careers, maybe we hit some artificial ceiling that we cannot seem to get around.

Maybe our gender, beliefs, or color of our skin has become more of an issue than our ability to contribute. While we'd like to think our society is more advanced than this, the data sadly shows we have a long way to go. Or maybe the disabilities we were born with make it difficult to contribute at a "typical" level - whatever the heck that is. For some (like me), these disabilities can result in our frustration tolerance, being overwhelmed and not able to stay calm to appease others. Maybe you are later in our career, where it can be difficult to get a job elsewhere due to ageism (again, wish we were further along here, but we aren't). Many of us at this point choose to suck it up and keep plodding along until 67. Or maybe you don't identify with these situations and have another one going on for you.

Whatever it is, and wherever you are in your career, building up resilience skills will help you. These are evidence-based and science-backed skills, and aren't just about being nice or staying positive. Some of these can be skills that some naturally have through their genetics or upbringing. Because of this, things can seem "easy" for them. However, for those who struggle, specific situations can feel insurmountable. So, for most of us, building up these skills helps not just with coping and mental health but with career progression.

These chapters will go through a variety of skills. Some may seem applicable right away, while others may have you asking, "WTF is Chris talking about?" One great way to use these chapters and skills to your advantage is to consider them like a giant buffet. If you don't know what something is, try a small amount. If you don't like it, there's plenty of other dishes (skills) you can try and enjoy. Also, over time, like our food tastes change, our needs (and abilities) to adopt and build skills change. So, come back to the buffet occasionally for a quick refresher or to retry a dish.

I'll go through common BS issues. You will probably identify with many as work patterns you have seen. I'll also walk you through a set of skills you can use to help detangle work poo. As you begin to use these techniques, you may define some "go-to" skills that work best for you (or work best in certain situations). After I go through these situations and skills, I'll then walk you through some ideas on how to create an architecture or approach that may serve you best.

Here are the common BS issues I have found set most people off and will cover in these chapters:

- Waste

- Group Think
- Problem Admiration
- Risk as an Excuse
- Toxic Hero Culture
- Me Me Me Syndrome
- Shiny Object Syndrome
- Wrongful Accusation
- Yes-people and Brown-nosers
- Over Celebrating
- Excuses
- Ethical Issues
- Pretending It's Okay

Here are skills you can learn, develop, and use to your advantage in these BS situations:

- Smash
- Curiosity
- Speak With Purpose
- Plot Your Trajectory
- Exercise
- Vent
- This Is It
- Meditation and Visualization
- Get Them To Problem Solve
- Follow the Customer

- Draw a Picture and Use Insights
- Networking in the Clicky Clicky Age
- Confront the BS Head-On

As one more suggestion, you may flip through some sections faster than others and come back to others. Any way you want to do this is fine. Enjoy the buffet here (it's all you can eat)!

CHAPTER 13

BS Issue - Waste

One thing that's especially difficult for me is to have a movie playing in my head of a customer's story of struggle. When I personalize these customers and take on their needs, wants and struggles it actually makes it harder to be at work meetings.

Wait what? Isn't that a good thing? Shouldn't we always focus on the customer's voice and needs when looking at things we do?

Well, yes, but know that when you go there, it will be nearly impossible to see inefficient junk and flat-out waste. And, if you look objectively, you'll also see some of that in your work patterns. Ouchy.

Customer Empathy

Let's use the example of a larger company that serves a bigger population on an ongoing basis. This could be retail, finance, car insurance, health insurance - it doesn't matter. Now, as a concerned employee of this company, you choose to actually listen to your customer's calls. You also look at the data from the support website, chatbots, and maybe some industry reports. Like most companies, you probably can identify improvements. And, if you get especially passionate, you'll remember a few outraged customer calls and want to solve their issues.

Maybe if you are in healthcare, you listened to a call of a single parent with a sick kiddo. They are trying to make ends meet, unsure of their finances, and getting the runaround from both the doctors and insurance companies. They are scared and angry. Maybe you even identify with them not being that far off from where you would be in a similar situation. Let's say this parent was trying to pay a $1000 monthly insurance bill and a lot of out-of-pocket medical office expenses due to the doctor's office not coding their work correctly with the insurance company. The doctor's office blames the insurance company and vice versa. The single-parent customer here is in the middle, with a sick kiddo and tough financial circumstances. Gross.

Meeting Waste

On the same day as that call, you're in a large company meeting. This meeting and its topics have been going on for a long time - maybe decades. The meeting has a structured agenda that was set weeks (or months) ago. The meeting is one-way and caters to a few loud people good at being loud. Often, the same issue is brought up again during this meeting. In that meeting, the lack of funds or resources to solve this issue could be brought up.

Using your super hyper customer focus, you look at the list of attendees. There are over 40 people on this call. Using a little math and people's titles, you put a price tag on this meeting at $7800 - or yearly at $93.6k. It's about 720 hours, not including prep and interruption time.

To add to your potential aggravation building here, the request to make a few things better (for people like the parent you listened to) has an estimate of 400 hours to complete. There's a slurry of excuses as to why nobody on any of their teams has the hours or resources to carry out this task.

To be a bit blunt here, if we look at this through the lens of that customer - the company is choosing this inefficient meeting that they have the resources for over the customer's needs. Yes, this is exaggerated. And yes, there is importance in a cadence of information meetings at most organizations for many reasons. And yes, there is likely some waste here as well.

Report Waste

> *"It's just we're putting new coversheets on all the TPS reports before they go out now. So if you could go ahead and try to remember to do that from now on, that'd be great."*
>
> — ***Bill Lumbergh, Office Space***

Another example of waste I hear often revolves around excessive status reports. Usually, the corporate weekly report cycle, even if the company has the best data visualization dashboards on the planet, goes something like this:

1. Create a Word or PowerPoint document with things that went well and things that didn't.
2. Circulate this up to your manager, then your director
3. The director filters and combines these and circulates this up to their VP

4. You can add your favorite movie music score here if you like… I use Indiana Jones.

5. The VP circulates it to their SVP. They may make changes, or their administrative assistant does for them.

6. The total package is sent to a C-level executive. It may also be sent back to everyone in the company.

7. Lots of questions are asked for more detail, often by the VPs or C-levels.

8. Questions are responded to and packaged in a way that better pleases the C-level. If something is unpopular, there's an action plan to make it more popular (for the C-level).

9. Little changes, and the same actions continue.

10. Rinse and repeat. Maybe play the Darth Vader theme now.

This cycle normally goes along with existing project-level meetings (with reports), financial budget-level meetings (with reports), divisional meetings (on the same topic), maybe an audit (hey look, a report), and likely a new leader that wants to see things a certain way (ooh, reports!).

At some point, just the engine of status reports creates a massive overhead and a life of its own. They can also become a "sacred cow" that nobody will call out or make it better. We just all "baa" along or, even worse, spend our precious energy complaining about it with no action.

Along with the status report dance, you may experience some more overt waste at your company. Things may be put into landfills that could be recycled. You feel your gut tightening, knowing they will be there for decades, but you also don't know how to bring this up without being shunned. You may notice overuse of print materials mailed out (and then thrown away or recycled). These mailings may not only be ignored but result in more confusion and more inbound calls, costing even more money.

Whatever waste you experience at your company can take a toll on your stress levels. You may have a background job in your brain running thinking about this and not even be aware of it. One thing is for sure: when you connect the corporate waste to a story from a customer struggling, it is difficult to let go of until you can take some meaningful action.

In the past, I asked a senior executive to help mentor me on this problem because I just couldn't get over it. Her advice was telling, "I can't help you." She meant that this caring and this level of customer championing is what we all should be doing. That frustration and care is critically important to the organization, even if they don't yet know how to act on it.

So, I know it's uncomfortable. Stay with it. We'll cover ideas and skills to make some progress here - for yourself and your company. The voice of your company's customers matter, along with your actions to champion them.

CHAPTER 14

Skill - Smash

"We must learn how to explode! Any disease is healthier than the one provoked by a hoarded rage."

— *Emil Cioran*

"Jeanine Smash" joked one of my co-workers when we were dealing with a particularly difficult situation. While we all laughed about this, as she emulated the Hulk, we also could all relate, as smashing something sounded pretty satisfying. No, not to hurt anyone or damage something, but just to get the frustration out. As a team, we were in a somewhat helpless work situation. Now, like all skills, this might be one you use a little, a lot, or not at all, so stay with us for a moment if you don't identify as a smasher.

This is a technique to use strategically after an event. We aren't advocating that you go all Hulk on your co-workers and create a scene. Yes, I know that's tempting sometimes, especially if you aren't green and built like Lou Ferrigno (yes, that's old school).

The structure of this technique is designed to help release pent-up frustrations and help let go of them – or at least the energy around them. This is more of a release valve and may not change the source of the core frustrations. However, there's a time when getting rid of this is important to your mental health.

For many of us, letting go like this can be scary. Will we become wild animals and not be able to control ourselves? Will we accidentally go off when we shouldn't? Will we harm ourselves or others? Done right, the answer to these is no.

What's important to use this skill is structure, time, place and safety. Some examples of this technique include:

- Smashing a bag of ice in a pillowcase on your garage floor.
- Getting inexpensive ugly plates at a thrift store and smashing them on that same garage floor (and then cleaning them up).
- Lifting heavy objects, maybe during a workout, and imagining the frustrating thing as you grunt through the exercise.
- Going for a walk or run and maybe stomping harder or sprinting for a short time as you imagine the frustration being squished by your shoes.
- If you know how or know someone who does, board breaking can be powerful. Please work with a pro here! It is powerful to write the obstacle you are breaking through on one side of the board, and the result or outcome on the other side. However, if you attempt this without the proper technique, you'll be visiting the ER with a broken hand.
- In reviewing these ideas, you'll likely come up with some of your own. As you can see in the examples, it's important to:
- Set up an environment (and time) to do this.
- Have the space (like a garage) that's easy to clean.

- Tell your loved ones, roommates, and others what you are doing. They may laugh (so what), or they may join in (yay). This may help stop them calling the padded wagon for you.
- Give yourself time to clean up - if needed for your smash.
- Visualize the frustration. Visualize breaking through it. Then see it doesn't have a hold of you anymore.
- Keep this small. If you need to deal with a major issue like a lifelong trauma, deep-rooted abuse, or anything close to that - please work with your favorite mental health pro before using smash as a tool.

Now, some have succeeded with Smash by visualizing smashing events. If that works for you, great. For me, something about taking physical action here is powerful and helpful.

You may have also heard of something called a "Rage Room" - a place where you can pay to go smash things. Sometimes, they even hold group events. While you can explore these, you can probably use things you already have or make inexpensive investments (ice bags, old plates, run, lift) to get the same results.

Just so you know Smash isn't just having a tantrum; there's solid science around this approach:

- "Breaking objects triggers the release of endorphins." (19) So, instead of releasing the Kraken and having an inappropriate outburst, you are helping your body "alleviate pain, lower stress, improve mood and enhance your sense of well-being." (20) Nice!
- When we feel powerless or unable to take meaningful action, smash can help us feel powerful. While this might

sound touchy-feely, this can do wonders for our self-esteem and not feel like things are being done to us.

- Prolonged exposure to something you interpret as stressful can flood you with cortisol and adrenaline. While this is a super useful cocktail for fight/flight type situations, swimming in these chemicals is harmful. Fortunately, Smash can be part of a cathartic release and you don't have to drown yourself in adrenaline. Researchers have found (21) that "The physical or emotional release that comes with catharsis can help you clear your mind, leaving you feeling calmer and more focused."

So, let's walk through using this tool with an example of waste we talked about in the last chapter. And, if this seems silly, that's okay. Let's say you work for a company that engages in death by status report, and you are aggravated by it. You are providing multiple status reports to multiple people, and it's hindering you or your team doing real work. Maybe nobody reads about the issues you put in your status report. Or maybe you see the inefficiencies people have by typing things in PowerPoint and not using your company's analytic tools instead. Whatever it is, let's pretend that is happening, and you are finding yourself with a shorter fuse to tolerate the madness.

In this example, let's also assume that later you will think of some ideas to change this or encourage the change, but right now, you are drowning in frustration, along with the cortisol and adrenaline, and need to let it go.

The next time you are at the grocery store, you buy a bag of crushed ice. You let your loved ones know that you are doing a thing and you are okay. You back your car out of the garage so you have plenty of space and put the ice in an old pillowcase. Then, you maybe put some music on your device with some headphones in your ears.

For a moment, imagine the annoying status reports. This should be easy because they are already poking at you. Then, smash the ice. If you can't lift it over your head and pound it on the ground, don't hurt yourself! You can also just use less ice. The first few times may feel weird, and you might think, "What if people are watching me?" Stay with it. At least 5-10 good smashes will help. On the upside, you probably want to limit your smash session to 3-4 songs (15-20 minutes). You might be tired before then.

As you are cleaning up, feel the tension leave your body. Tell your brain you don't need to think about status stress right now. You can access it later if you need to, but you are taking a break for now.

And, if someone watches or sees you, you can tell them you read about this in some bullshit book. You might find they want to try it on their own and get rid of their status mayhem in their mind. If a padded van shows up, we never had this conversation.

In all seriousness, Smash can be a powerful tool to relieve anxiety and stress, so we can imagine possibilities to fix things. When we are so overwhelmed with an issue, it's easy to feel stuck, helpless, and not able to ideate solutions. Smash is your friend.

Remember, as you use Smash, remember what Uncle Ben says in the Spiderman movies ""with great power comes great responsibility."

CHAPTER 15

BS Issue - Group Think

Ah, the herd mentality, it's so great for... herding animals. "Let's get everyone together so everyone can have input on the new project."

Wow, that sounds great. Everyone gets to have input; we hear diverse backgrounds and have a better idea because of our variety of talents and backgrounds. That will lead to a better product, right?

Not usually because of how most organizations execute these "collaborations".

Remember how your last meeting with over 20 people in attendance was? How many people talked openly? How many even could? Have you done the math here on what it would mean for everyone to share, let's say, 7 minutes of their feedback and expertise? For example, a team meeting of 20, that's 140 minutes (or over two hours). And that's if Bob and Brenda don't go all chatty like they usually do, right? More likely, everyone contributing here would push this meeting into three hours or more. These sorts of meetings are often shorter, and the attendee list is much larger than 20. This is just not set up to be collaborative.

Then, there's the peer pressure and group pressure. Let's say you have a new and different idea. Do you bring it up and disagree in public? Is it worth the political risk? Can you deal with the verbal and non-verbal backlash? Do you want to be known as "that person"?

Because of these pressures, innovative, divergent, or "out there" thoughts and feedback rarely are shared in these sorts of sessions. The inclusion of everyone here will probably result in the exclusion of many new ideas - the opposite of what this supposed collaborative meeting had in mind.

And, just to be a little challenging here to group norms that have formed - is everyone in that meeting qualified as experienced or directly exposed to this topic to add value? For example, I'm 100% *not* qualified to be on a medical panel, in the joint chief's staff meeting, or in a NASA rocket meeting. I don't have the expertise, nor am I directly exposed to this topic. Those are easy examples but the ones in most workplaces are harder. We want to say we have been inclusive - even if the structure only encourages the loud and repeat of the same (often failed) ideas.

A lot of the "include everyone" mantra comes from manufacturing, where line assembly employees were ignored or not properly included. They had direct experience and expertise, and would be affected by changes. They likely could contribute ideas that perhaps engineers, sales or finance hadn't yet heard. That collaboration, in small teams or even 1-1, could be useful and powerful. But putting the whole factory floor in a meeting for an hour and asking for new ideas might not give the results this firm would look for.

Something to consider here with groupthink is that new ideas are not just going against a single RAS (that part of the brain that plays the greatest hits on high rotation), but they are going against a herd of them. Imagine 20 sheep saying "baa" at the same time when sharing a new idea and you'll get an idea of the noise going on in people's brains. It's loud, confrontive and new ideas can be seen as a threat to the stasis (and the illusion of safety). They are quietly saying, "Don't make it harder" - even if what you are sharing would make it easier. Just plod along and get through the day. Don't rock the boat. Baa.

Now, these situations can become very frustrating and will probably lead people who care a lot to have an outburst (or an implosion). Usually, if this happens, the focus is on the person and the outburst. They have a behavior problem, right? Let's focus on that. Everything is fine with us, so the issue has to be them. However, if we look behind this outburst, there might be something useful. Maybe this comes from weeks, months or years of the organization not getting it. At the same time, this individual is trying to share practical solutions that would help, and not being heard. That would be maddening.

Now, outbursts aren't fun or nice, and I'm not advocating for shouting matches and temper tantrums as the best practice here. However, maybe looking behind outbursts and not villainizing the person brave enough to show emotion and a dissenting opinion is important.

Years ago, at an unnamed employer, I was listening to a contracting firm tell us about a solution for a complex issue. That issue was that an engine used for processing complex pricing wasn't scaling well. It was designed over 12 years ago, and the company had grown greatly. This tool was the special sauce for this company. Even with its age and clumsy interface, the pricing people loved it. There were technical tenants that I won't bore you with too much here, but I need to share some background to give some context. In software, there can be interpretive code and compiled code. Interpretive code looks like something you can read. At run time (think when you clicky click), an interpreter looks at the code, and then translates this into 1s and 0s for your computer to use. While interpretive code allows a lot of visibility and ease, it's not particularly fast or good for complex things. Think of someone speaking French. Then, a translator converts French to Spanish. Then, a person who speaks Spanish and English translates this to English. While it might be fun to listen to, the French-to-English translation rate here is slow.

So, why not use a universal translator or go from French to English directly? That's sort of what compiled code does. Here, you start with something mostly human readable. Then, you use a compiler that converts the readable (human) to the readable (computer). At clicky-clicky time, this code moves a lot faster, as it's not translating French to Spanish to English. It just goes.

Now, you are qualified to sit in any software engineering scrum. Mostly kidding here…

Okay, back to the story. So, yes, I was the outspoken person in this situation above. The existing code in the clunky system was all compiled (fast). Our volumes were going up, so we needed even more speed. The vendor was pitching interpreted code (slower by a lot). They did not budge on feedback around this being a concern. But this vendor had hundreds of developers they could bill out to us that specialized in interpretive (slow) coding. So, their solution served them with lots of billable hours to us, but not the customer or company problem.

This vendor was skilled in sales and relationship building and had many convinced that their way would work. I think if they shared that they could defy gravity on demand, some people would believe them. It was that bad. The technical team was quiet on this disparity. However, we looked around at each other a lot with "WTF" as we heard this absurd approach. What I also didn't know at the time is this vendor had a special relationship with my bosses' boss. So, other techies feared saying anything. They believed there would be retribution (and were probably right).

One day, in what was a final review meeting with this vendor, they were getting the group's approval before they pitched a multi-million-dollar, multi-year contract.

"This won't work," I started off in a frustrated voice. I had to actually interrupt them because I couldn't get a word in edgewise. The room went silent. It got weird. I had everyone's attention, so I continued with something like, "There's no way this will handle the throughput you are looking for and what the business needs are." The vendor countered, and I rebutted. While I didn't shout or drop the F-bomb, I am sure I was visibly angry. To be clear, I did suggest how to change their approach for it to work. So, I wasn't a total tool just complaining. However, I could tell that the focus was more on my "outburst" than the real issue. This company greatly valued conformity above all else, and I violated that.

One of the attendees let their boss know they were uncomfortable with my outburst. Then that person told someone else, and then some vague thing was said to me in a 1-1. Never was there any direct communication. However, this "incident" was held over me for the rest of my career at that company, even though this only happened a single time. Lying and fraud are okay, but honestly, it is not, got it. In that moment, I let my frustration get the best of me. I didn't yet have the tools that I'm talking about in this book. I feel awful that my words made someone feel uncomfortable. Let's be clear, I'm not suggesting being brutal, loud, angry or mean to share complex and important ideas.

However, I suggest that if you have one of these frustrated people, you take the time (maybe 1-1) to hear them out. You might even validate them with something like, "It makes sense that you would feel that way" (you don't have to agree with them, either). Then, ask them how they would solve it. Instead of a complaint mode, they are now sharing solutions that might be useful. Not everyone has the skills to easily do this or do it under duress. You may have lots of people knowing something will fail, but don't speak up out of fear for work culture norms. And, if your workplace doesn't entertain some dissent, or at least prototype alternative approaches, you are probably engulfed with groupthink and might just baa along with the herd.

If that comes across as harsh, life is just too precious and short to be mediocre. You have very limited time to share all of your gifts. In a group setting, we can still accommodate different ideas in a way that creates growth and makes things better. There is more to progress than focusing on compliance. It's a slight tweak and may take a little more effort. However, it is a lot more rewarding, fun, and more useful to your end customers than baa-mode.

CHAPTER 16

Skill - Curiosity

"Curiosity is the one thing invincible in Nature."

— *Freya Stark*

When we were young, we were all very curious. When we encountered something new, we would look at it, smell it, maybe even put it in our mouths. Later in life, we find ourselves less curious and may have decided how things are. Most of this is based on past experiences. Maybe we have decided that Brussel sprouts taste like small alien brains or that tomato seeds are scary. We could also quickly decide that some people are "our types" and others are not - without a single interaction.

At work, when we become frustrated about something or someone, it can be easy to blame someone. Often, this is in the form of somewhat villainizing a co-worker or manager. If only they did something different, or better, or less, everything would be fine, right? This is similar to *not* looking behind the outburst I mentioned earlier. We could react to that behavior with something like, "Chris has anger issues, and that's not appropriate." Most do. Or instead, we could be a little curious with "I wonder why Chris had that outburst, he seems really worked up. What else could be going on?"

The difference here is subtle and powerful. The first approach assumes that the other person has issues and should act differently in a way that is more soothing to us. Nothing wrong with that approach other than that it might miss some insanely great gems of information and opportunities for amazing results. The second approach is a little harder, but it's really not that big of a deal. With this approach, we need to handle the noise and abrasion of the outburst. We need to not take it personally, and look past it. We must assume the person showing that behavior would prefer not to be in this state. And then, we listen and understand. This approach takes time and skill to be sure. And, in our busy day, we can go to "I'm just too busy and don't have the time or energy for this."

The other thing that occurs in the second approach, while super subtle, is it actually soothes us, too. Our heart rate drops. Our fear of the other person (or fear of the noise of their outburst) goes down. Our breathing slows, and our threat response mechanisms also slow. In doing so, the problem-solving parts of our brain are more easily accessed. We may even build a relationship with this person we feared or loathed.

Sometimes, the BS has gone on for so long that getting to this state seems nearly impossible. We just don't want to take those steps and admit we might be wrong - or have some accountability. It's easy to say, "this sucks" or "they suck". It's hard to take accountability and action. No matter what choice you make in contacting the people at work that piss you off, scare you, or repulse you - there's a skill you can build without even talking to them.

Years ago, I learned this simple skill while a counselor at a camp. It seemed a little silly, but it was fun, and I could tell different parts of my brain were engaged. More recently, I used this with my son on the autism spectrum and found it calmed both of us down. It takes only a few moments and has interesting and immediate results.

Some of you may react to this skill as I did at first - "That's cute, Chris." You might not really put that much energy into it. That's okay. Others may use it more often for a time and enjoy the subtle difference it puts into the day.

We'll call this the Wonderment Process, and it has a few very simple rules to make it work best. You can do this by yourself, with another person, or a handful of people. One person will start off with "I wonder..." and, based on something they see, have a question. For example, if they are looking at a park and see a squirrel, they may say, "I wonder where that squirrel has been today." After a few seconds of silence (questions are not answered out loud), the next person goes with a different wonderment. This pattern continues for a few minutes until everyone has had 3-5 turns - or whatever is most comfortable. If you are doing this yourself, you can say it out loud or to yourself. What's cool about this exercise is that you can do it anywhere - in that annoying meeting, while stuck in traffic, or even in that longer grocery line (maybe speaking to yourself and not out loud in this case).

When we can get here, we are shifting the pathways in our brains. Instead of "they suck" or "this sucks," we are focusing on things we can be curious about. Different parts of our brain are engaged and may even start to answer these questions for you or make better movies in our heads. For example, your brain may make a movie of where the squirrel friend we talked about earlier has gone that day. Maybe they were on different trees, or running across a busy street, or napping after collecting food. Please understand this skill does not remove the issue at hand. Things may still suck. The traffic jam is probably still there. However, instead of being in agony in our own brains, we can create a different experience.

What do you mean, Chris? Traffic sucks, and I want to be angry about it and anxious. I know these emotions and like them. There should be no traffic for me because I'm important. I know. My brain tells me this, too, sometimes. Being "right" about the crappy situation is weirdly more comfortable than trying something new. Part of this is that RAS, with its heavy rotation top hits of "this sucks," playing. However awkward or silly it may seem, I encourage you to introduce your RAS to the alternative rock of the wonderment process.

For those of you who are parents, coaches or lead teams, this simple exercise can be great for team building and relationships. You may find that your kids, athletes or employees start this on their own as they learn it more. You will probably notice it requires one to be present, focused and calm for it to work best. You might even have interesting questions that you didn't expect.

I wonder what you'll come up with.

CHAPTER 17

BS Issue - Problem Admiration

The blue flickering fluorescent lights in the large conference room clash with the tiny bit of sunlight sneaking in through the window coverings. Paper shuffles around as large packets are handed out to the 30 participants in the room. Looking around, no smiles can be found. Some low-level grunts can be heard. Everyone looks tired and not very interested. The cheap copy toner makes the packets smell like burned popcorn in the microwave.

The presenter, reading the slides to the audience, walks through an extensive plan to update some systems that are out of date. The document's front page shows they have had dozens of reviews. The document then walks through a final state, what things will look like when complete. Then, the presenter walks through phases to get there. The document concludes with a staffing and financial analysis. The document introduces doing things differently. Instead of people logging into 10 systems to get their work done, they log into one. Instead of daily batch interfaces exchanging data, information is synced up in near real time. Some data and technology ideas are advanced for this organization but have existed elsewhere for decades. They are proven and sound.

Let's press pause for a second here. Have you been in a meeting like this in your career? Can you guess what will happen next? Is the presenter celebrated, congratulated, and does the team say, "When can we start"? In my 35 years in corporate America, I've sadly never seen that be the approach. What's celebrated instead is bringing up many risks - perceived or real - and reasons *not* to act. Perhaps, especially if the problem is large or well-known, the tendency is to observe it more but not to take action on it. Maybe even worse, the organization may choose an approach - a way of doing things - that makes it impossible to move the dial on this issue. They may go with a multi-year, multi-million-dollar approach with a giant team. Later, they will be surprised it wasn't successful and may even leave it halfway done, collecting more technical debt. They may blame the vendor, the project manager, the tech staff, or "the business" for the issues.

What rarely is looked at is the corporate disease I like to call "problem admiration".

This is a common ailment at every larger organization I've been at or talked to. People see things in their daily work that just don't seem right. Think about where you work and ask yourself a few questions:

- Are there systems (computer-based or human-based) that just don't seem to make sense?
- Are there certain job functions that seem like they aren't needed and are excessive?
- Do you see customer issues that need solving but nobody wants to address?
- Are there things considered too hard, so nobody wants to attempt a fix?
- Are there things that aren't talked about but are obvious issues?

For many of us, we can answer yes to all of these. The general corporate approach can be to assign a committee to address it. This body of people gets together and, you guessed it, admires the problem. They have a lot of meetings but rarely take any meaningful action. They'll probably even congratulate themselves on their "collaboration".

Problem Admiration is a clever disease, too. One of its variants helps make sure organizations rarely act. It disguises itself in fear of "duplicate action". This is the notion that we wouldn't want two parts of an organization to do the same thing. Instead, we should all meet, agree, and do things the same way (or do nothing). And, if we do this, we all share these amazing benefits, right? Sadly, these outcomes rarely happen. As much as they are talked about and seem like common sense, they rarely happen. And, if they do, the final solutions are so watered down they are nowhere near as effective.

For many years, I served in roles as a Technical Architect on projects. While this sounds very exotic (and sometimes can be), the ethos behind technical architecture at most organizations is simple. It goes something like this:

- Centralize everything.
- If you can't centralize everything, do it the same way, everywhere.
- Love all new technology and treat all old technology as bad.
- Complexity and layers are good.
- We can define everything with some boxes and colors on a page.
- Every solution is expensive, slow to get to, technically hard, and with results only in the distant future.

- Show a mythical end state of nirvana - but do not show any phases to get there.
- Everything should be real-time because that's always better.

Now, if you think that I'm against standards, normalization and best practices, my apologies, as this is not my point. At the same time, I must call this out. For most organizations, this approach has resulted in high costs, unsatisfied customers, continued technical issues, and continual problems. Technical vendors are experts here at sharing approaches that seem like they came from university studies. These approaches seem to make sense and can seem to be novel. But, if we zoom out, we notice they come in waves. For example, these are usually waves of decentralization then later, centralization. Once, at a conference, I heard a CIO tell a joke:

"A vendor told me to decentralize, and later to centralize, and we supposedly saved money both times."

The crowd roared in laughter… and gulped at the same time. In that moment, we collectively realized we were caught in the trap of problem admiration. The problem is rarely just the technology at play. The problem is the organization's ability to use it quickly to provide value to their customers and themselves.

Part of what makes the Problem Admiration disease thrive is larger groups. The thought is that including everyone or having everyone at the table makes things better. If that were true, it would have already happened. In his Forbes magazine article, Jacob Morgan writes "More people means more communication, more bureaucracy, more chaos, and more of pretty much everything that slows things down, hence why large organizations are oftentimes pegged as being so inefficient." (22) Morgan also shares a philosophy that Amazon has, that "if a team cannot be fed by two pizzas, then the team is too large."

Aside from this philosophy and the common sense of less is more, there are studies that back smaller teams helping prevent the spread of Problem Admiration:

Ringelmann Effect

Professor Maximilien Ringelmann did studies that showed that individual team members contribute less as the group they are in becomes larger. Some of his studies showed that a single person would give 100% of their effort to a task. However, this went down dramatically as more individuals were added. (23) More people resulted in less work being accomplished.

More people created lesser outcomes. Sound familiar?

Social Loafing

Social loafing is somewhat similar to the Ringelmann Effect, and Professor Alan Ingham adds more details. While there are ways to counter these effects, what the professor has found is that:

- Individuals exert less effort in a group task than when working alone.
- This can be due to less accountability and/or shared responsibilities.
- This is amplified when there's a group outcome and individual contributions are less defined.
- This leads to reduced productivity.

Social Loafing and the Social Impact Theory finds that "when individuals work collectively, social influence is diffused across group members, and each additional group member has less influence as group size increases. (24) So, while the intent of including everyone likely has noble notions and dreams of better outcomes, the very structure may do the opposite.

Creative Change

"If we all crave creativity so much, why do we reject new ideas so often?" — *Daniel H. Pink on the book by Dr. Jennifer Mueller*

Through several studies, Dr. Mueller "reveals how the implicit beliefs we have about effective collaboration (e.g., many hands make light work, two heads are better than one, and great leaders know the answers to problems) are inaccurate and can harm our ability to make collaborations work. My work shows that the mere act of collaborating can make people perform worse because they feel more confident than when working alone and so reject helpful outside advice." (25)

Whoa. So, we could even say that a corporate call to "let's collaborate" may be a call to not get anything done. Yikes.

Legos Study

In a study from UCLA, Penn State and UNC Chapel Hill, professors found that teams of four were almost twice as slow as teams of two (26). The study had participants build a structure, either with teams of two or teams of four. Given the collaboration and inclusion mantra for large meetings, we may be led to believe that the larger teams would do much better and produce a superior's solution, right? Not so. The team of four took nearly an hour to complete the task on average, while the smaller team of two averaged 36 minutes. While this is a simple experiment and one could certainly create a list of "yeah, buts." However, we also must acknowledge that a team half the size completed the work in half the time. Smaller was better.

What if the well-intentioned inclusion and collaboration doctrines, at least in their current forms, are failing to make companies more productive? What if making it "everyone's idea" makes the solution slower, less effective, and maybe not happen at all? These might not be popular or safe questions to ask in most work cultures, but the data makes it clear that smaller teams are more productive, effective, and faster. Maybe there's a way we can seek to be inclusive and diverse and keep smaller teams. Because there's no "safety in numbers" here. The long-term viability of an organization ignoring this is advocating for its own extinction.

CHAPTER 18

Skill - Speak With Purpose

In a packed room of teens on a summer day, Dr. Eric Jensen knew he had his work cut out for him. He not only had to educate, but he also had to entertain. Even harder, he had to get trendy teens stuck in being cool as their primary goal into listening to something unpopular and even taking uncomfortable action about it.

"Why did the dinosaurs die?" asks the dynamic Jensen, hopping about the stage. The students answered with "disease," "asteroid," "extinction". Eric energetically answers, "No, not that... they died because of dinosaur talk - rawr rawr rawr." Jensen animatedly shares that dinosaurs complained and whined a lot and agreed on things that "sucked" with other dinosaurs. Eventually, all that dinosaur talk led to their extinction.

Now, Jensen was making a poignant point here with this fictional and fun story. As far as we know, dinosaurs didn't talk that much (well, maybe raptors did). We have evidence that an asteroid had a major planetary impact in the past and was probably the source of their demise. At the same time, we also have evidence that negative stories and talk can affect our human perspectives and health. Sure, it can feel fun sharing that work WTF story with a friend and giving co-workers and bosses derogatory nicknames. The next time this happens to you with others, see how easy it is to say something positive about that person. Okay, it might be hard to find something about a person you despise, but for a moment, try. It's hard to do this when everyone is complaining and to feel safe doing this, right?

"We spend far too much time complaining about the way things are and forget that we have the power to change anything and everything." - Bozoma Saint John, Chief Brand Officer at Uber

When stuck complaining, you are a mixologist for a toxic cocktail for your body's systems. You've asked it to release stress hormones and divert energy. Dr. Travis Bardberry, an expert in this space, shares that "Complaining triggers your body to release cortisol, the stress hormone. Cortisol shifts you into fight-or-flight mode, directing oxygen, blood, and energy away from everything but the systems that are essential to immediate survival." (27)

Here's the thing - if we complain about something and do nothing about it, we are making victims of ourselves. This thing is now happening to us, and we are making ourselves helpless against it. Do we really want to have the things we cannot stand controlling us? Do we want to spend our precious life energy wasting time mentioning the things we don't like, even more? Now, I'm not suggesting that you make things up. You don't like this thing your boss or a co-worker did. That's real to you. You don't need to pretend it's not. But should you relive it 100x? Does that help you after the initial venting?

Now, we might not yet know what to do with this adverse situation. We also might get stuck with that dinosaur talk as a coping mechanism. It's almost like we are advertising "I don't like this" while silently saying "... and I don't know what to do about it."

But c'mon, what's the big deal, everyone does this, right?

According to many studies cited in an article by the Harvard Business Review, continual complaining has big effects on our brains (28):

"Through the repetition of bad, sad, mad and powerless feelings, the neurotransmitters in the brain can go through a neural "rewiring," which reinforces negative thought patterns, making it easier for unhappy thoughts to repeat themselves and leaving little room for the more positive feelings of gratitude, appreciation, and well-being. A continuous cycle of negative thoughts may even cause damage to the hippocampus, the part of the brain used for problem-solving and cognitive functioning. Over time, complainers become negativity addicts, attracted to the drama that comes with a complaining attitude."

Given our relatively short time on earth and the time we spend at our jobs, do we really want to be addicted to negative drama?

The Harvard article shares more about the ongoing effects of this:

"Chronic complainers also have a damaging effect on those around them. When people are thinking and reacting in negative and pessimistic ways, without realizing it, they transfer these feelings onto others in a process psychologists call "projective identification." It is as if they use other people as some kind of garbage can for their negativity, making these others feel weighed down and exhausted."

Before we go further here, let me be clear - if there's something illegal, amoral, abusive, unethical or anything that deep in your gut feels not right, you need to speak up about this. Speaking with purpose isn't about ignoring or pretending bad things aren't happening. Instead, it's choosing to act on them. When we choose to speak with purpose, we're engaging less with negative agreements and dinosaur talk. We are also choosing to act on what we complain about to make it better. Over time, this personal integrity is powerful and keeps us free from the drama and addiction that can occur if these behaviors are unchecked.

Now, lamenting about a single event or an issue for a short time differs greatly from endlessly going on and on about it. When overwhelmed by something, no matter how small, we sometimes need to just talk about it with someone we trust. We can also do things like create a structure around this stressor - give it a name, color, sound - which gives it less power and lets our brain package it up.

Let's go through an example:

"Can you believe what Jim said? He's such a cheapskate and tool?"

"Yeah, he's like the definition of a tool."

"I mean, we are a multi-billion-dollar company and growing, and he wants us to cut costs. WTF?"

"Yeah, and customers are all over us wanting more right now."

"What a tool."

Now, in this example, at least two people clearly think Jim is a tool. It sounds like he asked for cost-cutting ideas, and these two don't agree with that question or the intentions behind Jim's request. It also sounds like these two have concerns that the company is growing, and they won't be able to meet demands without some investments. With some interpretation here - it's also not likely they have communicated that to Jim. They view Jim as just a "cheapskate and tool." Let's exaggerate for a moment here. If we think that is all Jim is capable of, will we ask for or expect different behavior from Jim? Won't we somewhat want Jim to be that tool so it is a predictable story and in a weird way, safe?

Spoiler alert - yes, that is exactly what humans can do. It is also easy in this mode, to try to make issues someone else's problem, and have no accountability.

As John Mayer eloquently put it, here's the pattern:

"Me and all my friends

We're all misunderstood.

They say we stand for nothing and

There's no way we ever could.

Now we see everything that's going wrong.

With the world and those who lead it

We just feel like we don't have the means.

To rise above and beat it.

So, we keep waiting (waiting)

Waiting on the world to change."

Okay, if you don't want to wait for the world to change, what is the skill to learn here and how can we speak with purpose instead?

Let's first go with the definition from the experts at Quantum Learning who have been doing this for decades all over the world (29)

"Speak honestly and kindly—think before you speak to be sure your intention is positive, and your words are sincere. Words have the power to build people up and bring them down. They can uplift and enlighten or depress and destroy. You have complete control over the words you use, so choose them carefully. The first step is awareness. Think before you speak. Focus on communicating positives: strengths, praise, encouragement. Handle negatives carefully. Stopping to consider your intention before you speak is a powerful tool."

So if you choose to complain about something, what action are you also committing to? No more freebies here. From our example, what are we going to talk to Jim about? When will we explain our concerns and share our ideas to resolve them? How will we make this communication?

We may find we have lots of energy spent with others complaining about others. One way to interrupt this for yourself is to say (out loud or to yourself) "I'm really not ready to take action on this, so I don't want to talk about it." When the crazy comes up - whatever sets us off about these "tools" in our life - it's one million percent okay to acknowledge it isn't okay to you. It's okay to vent about it a couple of times. After that, choose to either act or let it go.

You can combine this skill with the Wonderment Process, too. Now, this will require some new effort and you may think I'm even crazier than you already do. However, if you are brave enough to try it, it could look something like this after you have cooled down from the event:

"I wonder why Jim said that."

"I wonder why Jim is so concerned about money."

"I wonder if Jim knows some things we don't."

"I wonder if there is some way I can help."

Flashing back to the story with the mythical Jim the tool, which is loosely based on a previous boss and some negative language I not so proudly used about him - it turns out there was a reason for his actions. The company we worked for was about to go through some serious merger activity. There were calls to reduce staff if costs cannot be reduced. Leaders could not share this detail because the company was publicly traded. Jim was looking for ways to spend less on things - software licenses, equipment - so he did not have to lay off people. He cared about his people and their livelihoods.

Yes, Jim's skills at relaying this message were not the best. And no, he didn't have the best relationship with his staff. Yes, maybe Jim could clue them in to what was going on without telling them. But Jim was also actually trying to protect their jobs and their incomes in this scenario. Maybe he was also a cheapskate, and maybe he was a tool - but he was also actually trying to be a good leader and keep the team employed through a tough time ahead. Yeah, that was a big gulp (not the drink) for me and greatly shaped what I thought about Jim and how I treated him afterward. His name isn't Jim, but the situation really happened at a previous employer, and we sadly used those names for him. Very lame on our part. Not a proud moment at all.

The other part of speaking with good purpose is poignant. Do your best to try to call out one positive quality about this "tool" you are complaining about. Again, don't make things up that aren't true, and don't pretend you aren't perturbed. This is not about lying to yourself. There may even be people that you struggle with saying anything remotely positive about. But, for most people, we can come up with one or two things.

In Jim's case, he was careful, willing to ask hard questions, and supportive of his staff financially during reviews. We later learned he was protective of adverse events happening to us. While there were parts of working with him that felt like micromanaging, he gave his young staff a lot of freedom with technical choices that were more expensive than he expected. While none of us knew it, he quietly dealt with his leaders, giving him a hard time about this spend.

While I rarely saw eye to eye with Jim, his character is outstanding. After several hard life realities and poor choices, Jim gave me many positive references. These references greatly helped my career get back on track.

Thanks, Jim! And sorry, I was really the tool.

CHAPTER 19

BS Issue – Risk As An Excuse

"The greatest hazard in life is to risk nothing".

– Steve Jobs

At most medium to large organizations, there's some process to mitigate risks. For some, this formalized risk management can feel like a new thing. For others of us, we can feel like there is a lot more of it. As it turns out, risk management is an old practice, at least in human terms. Risk management may date back to ancient Rome (30). Back then, there were mutual aid and "burial societies" that are "considered the precursors of modern insurance companies." There's also evidence later in history (but still very old from our current perspective) of two mathematicians (Pascal and Fermat) who "wrote to each other about games of chance in the 1600s, a correspondence that is believed to have given rise to modern probability theory used today."

Okay, so risk practices and the math around things like games of chance and insurance aren't a particularly new concept. But is it growing? A study from IMARC (International Market Analysis Research and Consulting Group) suggests that risk management functions are growing substantially (31). According to this study, the risk management "market size reached US $12.0 Billion in 2023." They also predict a steady rate of growth and the market going up to $35.9B by 2032. We live in a world of big numbers now, so to put the current $12B in spending in perspective, that's larger than the annual revenues of companies like Chipotle, Puma, and Airbnb. When it expands to $35.9B, this spending will be more than McDonald's, most major airlines and giant software companies like Salesforce (32).

Okay, so risk management isn't new, and it isn't small. It would seem like protecting against risks is a good thing for companies, right? It would please our risk-adverse RAS that's playing the top hits "that's scary" and "that's new, don't do it". Before it seems like I'm suggesting abandoning all risk management programs, and it's the BS bastion of all things bad in corporations, in balance, risk management is important.

The volume and impacts of cybersecurity breaches, for example, is on the rise (28):

- A major European IT services firm found that the number of victims of cybercrime has gone up a lot. "Since 2001, the victim count has increased from 6 victims per hour to 97, a 1517% increase over 20 years." (33)
- About 1 in 5 internet users are affected by nearly 1 Billion emails exposed per year
- Data breaches cost businesses an average of $4.35M in 2022
- 55.35M US citizens were affected by cyber-crime in 2022

Risk management can help make jobs safer, companies more prepared, provide the ability to handle unexpected events, and potentially even save overall time and effort. And when it becomes out of balance, it can be an issue. Generally, risk management programs have some intake for new projects or issues. They review what impacts these actions could have on the organization or how it maps to internal policies. There may also be federal, state or local laws that the risk management teams need to adhere to. Because of this there may be legal reviews involved as well. Certainly, the company doesn't want to be at risk of violation of these laws or statutes. Nor does any company want to put customer data at risk of breach.

To put this in numbers, the same study mentioned found many more staggering facts about data breaches (34):

- Data breach costs have gone from $2054/hour 20 years ago to $787k/hour today.
- There are nearly 97 data breach victims every hour.
- 76% of respondents in a 2022 case study covering the US, Canada, UK, Australia and New Zealand say their organization has suffered at least 1 cyber-attack this year.

There is great potential in risk, privacy and compliance programs to help prevent issues like this. However, out of check, there are other issues these systems can create. For example, what's the incentive for these teams to find a way to say yes? Here, I'm talking about high-integrity ways to find a way for a new project, tool or function to succeed within the bounds of the rules. This is not to suggest we go manipulating or pretending, but address things head-on and find a way to yes. Is there any incentive, other than just executive pressure, for these risk organizations to say yes? And, when things fail or break, is it the risk organization at fault or is it the business unit that accepts the risks?

Often this important role does not have the same incentives or motivations as the rest of the organization. These can be seen to be combative, but they don't need to be. As an example, customer service functions face the customers' needs on the front lines and must answer them directly. Similarly, sales functions must hit numbers or leave the company and have direct accountability to this. Project functions have limited funds and dates to hit milestones. Most executives are held accountable for some key performance indicators for profit, loss, customer satisfaction and employee satisfaction. However, usually risk programs are insulated from this and have few incentives to say yes. They do, however, have many reasons to say no.

One thing that can be missed here is that choosing *not* to do something, even if it has a risk profile, also has a risk. This is how companies can become extinct quicker than you may expect.

Not long ago, Kodak was the king of film for cameras and processing. Kodak started in 1892. It survived multiple wars, major recessions, and numerous depressions in the economy. What some also don't know is that Kodak developed the first handheld digital camera in 1975. Internal Kodak documents from 1979 showed that many believed that all cameras would be digital by 2010. However, executives decided against going digital for several risk-related reasons (35).

While Kodak executives waited, along came digital cameras. Many other companies explored early adoption here. Kodak waited. At the time, digital photo technology was inferior to film in resolution. Digital devices were much more expensive than film ones. Even worse, digital cameras then would only take a handful of images at a time and could take hours to upload to a computer.

They didn't yet have large screens to see if the image was great or not, so you had to upload it to a computer to find out. On the surface, it sounds like the Kodak executives made a good choice, right?

Film cameras were inexpensive and dominated the market. But, before long, we all had smartphones that could take high-quality images for "free" (no film processing). We are now used to instant gratification and no costs to take multiple photos to get the best shot. While Kodak tried to catch up in the mix of this, it was just too late. After suffering major losses, Kodak has recovered from bankruptcy and still has a business focused on film for motion pictures. It still has 4000 employees and $1B in revenue. However, this is a far cry from the 20,000 employees it used to have, and the market dominance it enjoyed.

No, a single decision wasn't the cause for Kodak's demise. But did the risk of not acting in 1979 or taking enough action, have proper treatment? Based on what we see today, likely not.

I share this story because it's easy to feel safe when you are in a big, old, established industry. It's also easy to see new approaches as risky and see taking no action around them as the smartest play. Truly, sometimes, this is the right play. But be careful, you could also find your company being the next Kodak.

Let's go through three stories - that might sound all too familiar to you – where risk can be misused as an excuse not to act at all.

Risk/Reward Ratios

In a large conference room, the VP of the Project Management team proudly told a C-level executive his next steps. He confidently said that he would analyze all the options and pick the least risky one.

The room went silent. The exec had a look on this face. You could see the gears churning. I could tell he was making his word choice carefully. His body language indicated that he disagreed. "No. We may pick the highest risk one if it produces the most value and fastest time to market. Risk is important but not the only thing. The lowest risk one might be the worst choice for us."

This statement shook up the project teams. The whole mantra of some project management approaches is to look at risk/reward ratios and use that math to pick the "best" effort. Unchecked though, this misses the risk of not doing something and could lead to the wrong "Kodak moment".

The Innovator's Curse

On a more personal front, if you are an innovator in a larger organization, you likely have encountered multiple steps of approval. Along with a business case you had to get approved and somehow get funding for, you also had to line up staff or a consulting firm to do the work. You may have had to do an RFP for new software and/or services. There will be many contracts that require legal and procurement review. There's also likely an information security review and technical architecture review. After these, you may find privacy, risk, or compliance reviews at the end. After all these reviews and phase gates, after overcoming and modifying so many things, after all this due diligence, you can still be met with a "no" here by a risk team. Remember, often, these organizations have no accountability to customers or profits. They may not even have accountability if there's a breach event. They may not fully understand the complex business problems you are solving. Sometimes, these points cannot accurately be "one-paged" with bullet points for the intake to this team.

Once more, you may care deeply about this new effort and have personalized its success with your own. Let me share a story from a colleague that might sound like a TV script, but it's the reality for many projects in large to medium organizations.

Approval Quagmire

Carl was the point person for a large software platform in which his company invested millions every year. While the company got a lot of value out of this software, it was also a target of complaints. Some of that reputation is because little staff were funded to work on the software platform, so it was tough for them to make progress and keep things up to date. This relatively tiny staff was not motivated to use the best practices from this tool's vendor – they were trying to stay afloat. To make it worse, some parts of this platform the company paid for were not yet approved by the compliance team. Major parts of these software licenses, which the company spent millions on, sat idle. These were not part of what internal teams could use. They were bundled from the vendor, so Carl's company just couldn't spend less on the parts they could use. Peers to Carl's company used these tools successfully and did not have compliance issues.

What did these tools do? Peers of Carl's company used these tools to create better employee experiences and better customer experiences. The tools used some basic (now) artificial intelligence (AI). The tools would look at what similar customers or employees do in a situation and make these suggestions to the end user. This would greatly help new employees just starting in this complex organization. This would also help customers understand complex issues and even reduce some of the company's customer service costs.

Carl's team was excited about this. They haven't been this motivated in a while. They took free courses from the vendor and did prototypes in their non-production environments. The business units were excited, too. When they went to deploy this technology, they learned it required a different agreement and wasn't approved for use yet. So, Carl began the process to gain this approval. He obtained business unit approvals, which took weeks and lots of back and forth. Ultimately, others arrived at the same conclusion Carl had. His culture rewarded second-guessing, so Carl had a lot of this in his process. Carl then had technical and information security reviews. Now remember this platform, although his company spent millions on it, was not a favorite. Parts of the organization preferred to build everything themselves instead of using platforms like this. Carl used to joke they would never buy a car from a car dealership but would create their own assembly line and make their own cars instead. This made Carl less popular, although he was probably right, and his joke hit too close to home.

Carl finally obtained technical and information security approvals. Meanwhile, the vendor introduced some technology that made this use even more secure. While Carl's company moved slowly, the industry didn't. Carl talked to another peer company in the same space, and they deployed this technology three years ago with great success.

So, even though it's a technology used by a peer, matches all the needs of the company, and has about every review possible, this should be a slam dunk for the compliance teams to share their issues, make accommodations move on, right?

As you probably guessed, there were delays. People were "busy". Issues were "complex". Even better, no answers were never directly answered with a no... although they weren't yes. Ultimately, the risk groups wanted sign-offs from over 20 VPs and executives they also agreed with this approach. The timeline on all this wrangling, from the business case to finally having signed documents and the ability to act was over five years. Yes, five years. And no, this wasn't in the 60s; this happened in the late 2010s.

Carl was noticeably frustrated and consumed. The organization made it about his frustration and not their thorny process for innovators. Why was Carl so upset? Didn't he know this upset affected his peers and was inappropriate? Why couldn't he be composed all the time? His company missed that they may have been part of creating their own Kodak moment by introducing more delays to be "safe," while competitors had a head start on launching. Instead, they focused on Carl.

For some reason that defies logic - maybe just raw stubbornness - Carl didn't leave and stayed the course. He had to personally champion this effort, and it took a toll on his health, stress levels, and likely his upside potential at that organization. There are not many people like Carl who would keep plowing through this many levels of resistance in an organization. While we can celebrate that he ultimately "made it," this is not what risk organizations or cultures should do. Meanwhile, Carl heard from his peer organization they had a 20% reduction in some key costs (many millions of dollars) and an increase in customer satisfaction of 15%.

In comparison, in that same year, his company experienced a 5% increase in costs.

Clearly, the risk of missing out on this reduction in cost and increase in happy customers was not factored in his company's risk decisions. Those departments were incentivized to say no. Years later, thanks almost entirely to Carl's continued efforts, his company is attempting to catch up to their peers. As you might imagine, Carl has little incentive to innovate anymore, if he knows the struggle he must go through – again.

CHAPTER 20

Skill - Plot Your Trajectory

"Map out your future - but do it in pencil. The road ahead is as long as you make it. Make it worth the trip."

S— Jon Bon Jovi

When dealing with day-to-day stressors, it can seem overwhelming. That thing that your boss did again, or coworker did again or corporate initiative you think is stupid - those can create considerable upset and feel like there's a wall there.

Stop and zoom out.

Here's a quick exercise to help. It might not make sense at first. We'll connect the dots for you after this exercise.

Go to your favorite web browser and check the value of Bitcoin. If you type in "BTC price" in Google or Bing, you'll get a current price chart that looks something like this.

Throughout the day and even week, Bitcoin's price will seem volatile. Many never consider Bitcoin because it feels too volatile. However, that is a different book.

Just notice the variance on a shorter term - hourly, daily, or even during the week. Notice the emotions you may have about this - fear, anxiety, wanting to run, or starting a dialogue about it. If you like Bitcoin, you've got a story to tell about how great it is and how it will change the world. If you don't like Bitcoin, you may have a story about how it's dangerous and there are scammers, and how you should avoid it.

Just notice the stories, emotions, and reactions to the volatility.

Okay, now we will zoom out. Click on the 5 Year or Max buttons. You'll see something like this.

When we zoom out, the flux of the hour, day and week are changed. Over the life of this asset, it's up almost 13000%.

From that context, we might be saying, "Why didn't I get into this in 2010?"

We can also see some rise and fall patterns. Again, that's a different book, but I'll quickly share that Bitcoin has four-year cycles as part of its algorithm. Because of this, there's some expected volatility as these swells roll through. This isn't investment advice. Your mileage may vary. Brush and floss daily.

Joking aside, notice your emotion when you zoom out. Is it a doom and gloom one, or are you able to access dreams and strategic thoughts that are bigger picture?

Okay, let's connect the dots here.

When zoomed into something so closely, like an event of the day, it can feel volatile. We can feel stressed. Those emotions and reactions are real, and we don't need to pretend they aren't.

However, when we can zoom out and maybe look at our careers with a 5- or 10-year lens, where are we?

What are the many successes we have had? Where have we grown, changed, or overcome things? What sort of progression have we had - either in title, or pay, or type of work? What accolades or accomplishments have we enjoyed?

While you are zooming out, what do you want your graph to look like? Where do you want to grow? What will you be doing?

Course of Action and Manifesting

When we zoom out, the day-to-day issues can more easily be put in context, and we can see where this fits in our trajectory of where we want to go.

Absent of this exercise, we can feel stuck in some sort of doom loop that looks like this:

1. Events happen.
2. We don't like them, it stresses us out, and we don't know what to do with that energy.
3. We tell others and ourselves how much it sucks. We may exaggerate it.
4. Our energy becomes consumed with this activity, sometimes daily.
5. Without a "why" or a perspective check, we go back to step one and repeat this.

Now, because you are probably human, you have done this pattern (apologies to the aliens reading this for my speciesism). You probably have a spot in your life where you still do this pattern today. One quick note on this loop - it's similar to those who have experienced major trauma. Now, we can judge ourselves and say something like, "Why am I whining about this, it's nothing like this person that went through that gnarly life event." While the events might be different, how our plumbing reacts to it can be the same. It's the plumbing we were born with. If there's something your brain interprets as a stressor, even if you don't think it should be a "big one," your wiring has already made that decision. In that case, it gets filed under the major trauma that may require fight, flight or freeze.

Notice this isn't fight, flight, freeze, get over it, be open-minded, be patient, be calm, be Zen, be kind, be composed, and have the best response. Until we get over this stressor, our bodies react on autopilot. This is simply because, at that moment, we didn't have the skill to handle the stressor. It overwhelmed us. Not knowing this can set us up to blame ourselves or judge our reactions. That won't help.

If you watch sports, think of a few top athletes. I recently watched a documentary about the top tennis players in the world. These are elite athletes in insanely good shape. They have access to the best equipment, the best trainers, and premium coaches in the world. This often even includes sports psychologists to help with their mindsets. They make hundreds of millions a year. When they are at their best, it's awe-inspiring to watch them. Covered in sweat on a hot day, with a giant live crowd (and more watching on TV), they do small miracles like 150 mph serves. They do this for four hours at a time.

However, sometimes, these elite athletes get derailed. Something happens - either inside their head or on the courts - that overwhelms their stress response system. If they get stuck there, their play becomes rougher. This can spiral into being stuck and losing the match. Others, somehow, can experience this event, recenter and still play amazing. Now, they may lose the match that day still - but they will have done so by playing at their best and not emotionally losing it.

Most of us (again, aliens aside), likely don't play pro sports at this level. But our brains are wired the same. When an event happens, and we get stuck and stay there, we can doom our day, week or even year. We can wreck our match.

So, here's how you can use zooming out, along with the other tools in this book, to get recentered and focused when you experience that work BS:

1. Realize that day-to-day is volatile. Think of the Bitcoin example.
2. Zoom out. What are your accomplishments over the past 5-10 years? What have you already overcome that was gnarly?
3. Create a 5-year milestone – or remind yourself of one you already have.

We have covered the first two steps here, so let's talk about the planning step.

Start with this question: "If I were to be wildly successful in my career in the next five years, what would that look like?"

For a moment, resist the information about your circumstances - how smart you are, what degree you have, what job you have, where you live, how much time you have - just let yourself go to what wildly successful would look like.

Think of your title, who you would work with, what sort of work you would do, and what you would get paid. Think of your lifestyle - where you would work and what would you do outside of work?

And finally, give it the Sunday test. How would you feel Sunday evening going into work?

Now notice - we aren't focusing on the steps to get there, or how hard it is, or any of that noise right now. Zoom out and focus on where you want to be ideally. Tell the filters that say you can't have that they get to take 10 minutes off. Write this down or draw it. Even if it seems silly, or perhaps especially if it seems silly, write this down. Yes, this requires putting this book down and doing something. If you can't do that, make sometime later today or the next morning to make it happen. Even if you are an alien.

Now that you have this wildly successful vision, you will just be open to the possibility. Yes, this will seem woo-woo to some, and you'll think I'm full of BS. Whatever. What do you have to lose? You are spending hours a week bitching about work. Instead, we're talking about trying something for a few minutes. Worst case, you lose a few minutes. Best case, it's better.

Okay, so at least once a day, relive this dream. When the noise comes up that says you can't have it, tell it to take its coffee break. If you experience a lot of BS about it being unreasonable, say, "I'm open to the possibility of this." You will repeat this for about a week. If you miss a day, just get back on it the next day. After about a week of this, you have hacked your brain's RAS. Instead of the I can't hit on heavy rotation, there are at least a few messages about this being a possibility. Other parts of your brain may start to get creative and think about options to take next steps or how things could happen.

Your RAS is actually an awesome hunter-gatherer. It's like saying,, "Hey brain, go get me evidence of this to be true." If you let it go on autopilot, which most of us do, it may think it's to find more evidence about how work sucks. You'll get even more of those hit tunes on high rotation. Instead, let it know the music you want it to play.

This skill needs friends to do its best work. Yes, after you've done this little bit of mindset hacking, you must take some action steps. These are ideally small at first to help build up confidence. For example, you could research different roles available at your company, or how you could learn a new skill, or maybe what skills companies you admire are hiring for. You can also set aside 20-30 minutes a week to brainstorm with yourself about what next steps can be.

When you zoom out, you are going for both more useful contexts (how big is this really). You are also creating your future context and taking a few little actions to make sure you're navigating in that direction. Now, much like that price of Bitcoin bouncing all over, in the short term, you may experience that bouncing around, too. Some things won't work out like you hoped (shocker, I know). Others will be even better than expected (oh crap, I can't complain). However, with a new context, when you zoom out, you'll see some rather amazing long term gains worth celebrating.

As you do this, you'll know that the daily volatility can be like turbulence on a plane. It's uncomfortable, maybe even scary, but it will pass and not last forever.

The captain has turned off the seatbelt sign, and you are free to move about the cabin.

CHAPTER 21

BS Issue - Toxic Hero Culture

"Here I come to save the day!"

— Mighty Mouse

Who doesn't love a heroine or hero? They come and save the day and rescue us from bad things. This is epically good, right? Well, it makes for the highest-grossing movies, and we appreciate the many heroes in our life.

I can clearly remember a time in middle school (yes, in the dark ages) that a much bigger kid was about to beat me up. He had done this more than once, and I didn't have the skill to fight back very well. Out of nowhere, someone I hardly knew interrupted it. He was a big, powerful, popular kid, and everyone was surprised that he did this. He also let the bully know he would be in a world of pain if he ever did it again – and he never did. Decades later, I'm incredibly thankful that he stepped in and was a hero to me.

But the work hero culture I'm talking about here is quite different from my hero in middle school and the actors in the blockbuster movies. This pattern is where the organization refuses to address the root cause of some issues on an ongoing basis. Instead, this company celebrates those with duct tape and bubble gum that keep things afloat.

Rapidly developing and sometimes being sloppy to serve a customer or iterate to something better is much better than sitting around admiring problems. However, an ongoing culture where only heroic efforts are celebrated, and little is done to address the core issues is, well, toxic.

A lot of times, we use the word "firefighting" as an analogy for these activities. Let's go there for a moment. So, in the case of a real fire we have these amazing first responders that are called out to our rescue. At least one, and maybe two expensive rigs with trained professionals is now on the way. On the back end, a massive logistics effort handles the 911 calls and dispatch. In advance, fire hydrants and water systems will be in place for this fire. Several building codes and construction practices are in place to limit damage should fire occur. Because of this new emergency, the response teams cut through traffic, deploy special gear to keep them safe and begin tackling this emergency. To put out the fire and keep it from spreading, they will probably cause water damage to the house. Now, it would burn down without this intervention, so this isn't a critique, just a fact of what has to happen.

These hard-working people should be celebrated - all the time - for their amazing efforts. However, could you imagine what their jobs would be like if a few things weren't in place, and they had to respond to 10x or even 100x more fires? Can you imagine the cost, clean-up and disruption? Would we even be able to source that much equipment and staff without massively raising taxes to support this?

When I was doing research for this, I learned of the massive effort that is made to both prevent fires from happening and provide localized responses so a hook and ladder doesn't have to be deployed every time. According to the National Fire Prevention Association in the USA (36):

- Seven people die in home fires every day.
- Fire departments respond to an average of 355,400 home fires each year.
- Cooking appliances are the leading cause of home fires.
- 65 percent of fire deaths occur in homes without working smoke detectors.
- It takes only 30 seconds for a small fire to spread.

When we stop and think about it - these numbers would be much higher without a number of things in place. We have smoke alarms, training in schools, building codes, and so many other things to keep fires from happening. While these aren't as celebrated as the amazing first responders, they quietly are responsible for an even larger number of incidents not happening.

Shifting back to the workplace, for those of us who aren't actual firefighters, this translates well. If a workplace continues to focus on firefighting and celebrate those activities heavily, they will find themselves stuck there. The perhaps less exciting components of creating new processes, deploying new technologies or exploring new staffing models don't have theme songs or action figures. We won't see a TV show or movie series featuring their efforts. However, preventing these things from happening is where many companies can miss major opportunities. While it's great that people are there to put out fires, you end up with a trashed house and an expensive rebuild. It also burns out your staff over time.

Once, I was considered one of these heroes at work, quickly fixing broken things and often working the 2 am-4 am shift. This timing was due to systems having low activity and it being agreeable to have maintenance activities in the wee hours of the morning. Nearly all these sessions were to fix things that could have been caught with a tiny bit more testing or diligence. However, the company valued the "hook and ladder" more than the smoke detectors.

So, about every Tuesday and Thursday (early) morning, I was on a conference call with five of our largest customers. They were also up at 2 AM to make sure things were running smoothly afterward. I would have 2-3 staff online from my team and 2 on call ready to handle issues if needed. They were day shift staff, so this disrupted their schedule and that of their families.

Usually, these were smooth rollouts, and that was celebrated. We were the heroes. The company loved us, and we constantly got accolades. However, our suggestions for improvements, so we could not have to do this, fell on deaf ears. What the company also missed, along with this miserable employee experience, was the message it sent to its customers. After about a dozen of these sessions in a few months, all began to ask questions - rightly so.

At the core of these questions was - "why aren't we important enough for you to do better in the first place?"

On a large roll-out evening of new code, things went absolutely upside down. About five hours into this, I told my leader we had to back things out to make the outage window. He ignored me and, worse, started swearing at me. But swearing didn't fix the issue. He believed, not looking at the situation at all but his pride, that we could "fail forward". We had attempted that - trying to make fixes with bubble gum and duct tape - for the last two hours. It wasn't working. Staff were tired and starting to make more mistakes out of exhaustion.

As you might expect, my leader's choice of ignoring reality and hoping we could "firefight" more had a stunning effect. We came out of the outage window down. Our service level agreement was for 99.99% uptime, so in several minutes, we had major penalties to pay our customers. Finally, my leader agreed to fail back, much too late. We took about 4 hours to get things back to normal during the busiest time of our customer's day. Several million dollars were lost by our customers and the fines in our service level agreement were substantial.

After the dust cleared, you might think the company would want to take different actions to keep this pattern from happening again. Sadly, other than some wordsmithing to clients and apologies, this didn't happen. Even worse, the firefighting team correctly advocating to fail back and keep things whole was let go. I was part of that, and honestly, it was the biggest blessing ever to leave that culture. But they had repeated this pattern with other firefighters for the last five years.

As long as they could eke out a little bit of a profit, and save face, they kept going. This eventually caught up with them and they could not fight anymore. Most companies don't go as far with this as this one did, thank goodness. My recommendation is to balance the appreciation for your "first responders" with work issues with immediate and longer-term actions to keep these issues from happening again.

Now, when making progress, you will have issues and downtime as part of this progress. However, there are dozens of modern processes, systems, and best practices today to allow rapid development and deployment - and keep high uptime.

Celebrate the people and processes that keep things humming along as much as you celebrate the people who "save" the company from its own bad decisions!

CHAPTER 22

Skill - Exercise

"Chris, go walk the stairs!"

This simple advice, in context, was one of the best I've ever received from a leader - and I've been blessed with great advice from many leaders. I was dealing with a contentious business division. For months, they were obstructing some top priority items my team and I were accountable for. We had tried many tactics to get things resolved. In response, this other division put up barrier after barrier. It was almost like they were making up reasons not to do things.

Even more frustrating, I had performed jobs like this division in the past. While I could be empathetic, I also knew things didn't need to be so slow, expensive, or difficult. Lots of anxiety, anger and frustration were brewing inside of me, and I was not using any skills to remedy this. I probably told my wife and kids about it a dozen times and thought about it a hundred more times when not at work. As you might imagine, being this pissed off made it very challenging to stay calm and friendly in conversations with this business unit. And, while perhaps I shouldn't have to and they should get their stuff together, that's not the culture of where I chose to work. Being "disruptive" carried a higher negative weight than not acting efficiently. Yes, that's absurd, and it's the case in many large organizations. Over time, people generally give up and stop trying. I'm either not that smart, way too stubborn or care too much - so I kept going.

One day, noticing my frustration, my VP told me to walk the stairs. This took me back a little bit, but I did it. As I pounded up and down those stairs, I vented off a bit of my anger and frustration. Something about being physical with it helped me let it go. The next day, when the same situation reared its ugly head, I headed to the stairs. My VP was there, too. Apparently, this was a strategy he used as he dealt with the same frustration. We laughed as we briefly named why we were walking up and down. We grabbed a quick coffee afterward and went back to work.

Eventually, this situation was resolved. As I mentioned, I'm stubborn (or something). For a change, I was not totally trashed inside because of this situation. Just simply walking the stairs for a few minutes had a major positive impact. And, when I remember to do something like this, it always has positive results for me. Now, there's probably 8 million studies that talk about what we eat and how we move can help us have a better life. This isn't new information. And, even with this information, most of us have dozens of excuses as to why we don't do this. We may feel shame for not doing it.

Instead of rehashing this, I'm going to suggest some micro exercise to help with your work stress. This can be done in a few minutes, before or after a meeting, and just about anywhere. Now, let's be clear, you are doing this for you. It doesn't make whatever BS someone else is engaged in right. It doesn't resolve the situation. But it will help your health - mental and physical.

What's interesting is that when you do this, you may find a few new ideas pop into your head. When we find some calm and get out of fight/flight/freeze mode, we can access the problem-solving and creative parts of our brain more easily. Occasionally, they share a new idea or angle that may help move us forward. But even if this doesn't happen right away, you can let go of a lot of the junk you are probably clinging to.

Here are a few things to remember that might help motivate you to move instead of just pout when in that rut at work:

- A recent study by two UK universities found that "mood and creativity were improved by physical exercise independently of each other." (37) Interestingly, the study also found there was a "significant increase in positive mood after exercise (P<0.001) and a significant decrease in positive mood after video watching (P<0.001)."

- Similarly, a current Harvard Business Review article reminds us that "Exercising releases endorphins — chemicals our bodies produce to relieve stress and pain. When we are less stressed, our brains venture into more fruitful territory." (38)

- But, if you can walk in nature, even for a short time, it can produce exceptional results. According to a recent experiment in Japan, "those who walked in forests had significantly lower heart rates and higher heart rate variability (indicating more relaxation and less stress)." (39)

- A similar study in Finland found that "even short-term visits to nature areas have positive effects on perceived stress relief compared to a built-up environment. The salivary cortisol level decreased similarly in all three urban environments during the experiment." (40)

- The National Science Foundation found that "restorative influences of nature involve a shift towards a more positively-toned emotional state, positive changes in physiological activity levels, and that these changes are accompanied by sustained attention/intake." (41)

CHAPTER 23

BS Issue - Me Me Me

> *"Bees don't waste their time explaining to flies that honey is better than shit."*
>
> — *Thomas Banks*

Years ago, my father worked for a major advertising agency with a large toothpaste company as a client. In helping to launch a new campaign, they did a massive amount of research to see who was buying their product in volume. Instead of assuming who their target market was, they looked at actual purchase data. While this approach is common now in our digital age, this was unique to do in the 1960s.

After nailing down who was buying the products, then understanding what product they were buying, and going further to understand why they bought it, his team better identified their customers. In the marketing world today, this can be known as an ideal client or an ideal client profile. Professional advertising and marketing companies use this information to both best serve and cater to these clients. Many times, the data and insights can seem counter-intuitive to the wants and needs of those clients. However, focusing on the actual buying behavior can be much more successful than just what people say they are all about. For example, someone might say they are a health nut. But, when we look at their actual grocery list and gym attendance, there might be some variance there. They may be a health nut in many ways, and they may also frequently buy a product that doesn't match that. This can be missed if the actual buying behavior isn't used and only simple demographics like salary and location are.

So, after months of extensive research and testing, his advertising team was pitching a new approach to the executives of this giant company. They now had a massive amount of market information, which was new to this organization and targeted ad campaigns to reach these audiences (magazines, school programs, radio, and TV). Based on the data, they also had projections for new profits and opportunities that were significant. From what I understand, it was one of my Dad's most thorough presentations.

So, after all these well thought out efforts, what did the CEO say?

"I don't like it."

Yes, that was about it. The team was stunned by this and the silence in the room was deafening. After a few moments, a senior person on my Dad's team spoke up.

"Bill, I don't give a rat's ass if you like it or not. The data shows that people like you don't buy our product and these ads aren't designed for you."

Bill was not used to being talked to in that manner. The silence and glares intensified. Bill called the meeting to a close. My Dad's colleague expected to be fired, but thought it was the right thing to do.

A few hours later, Bill's office called to let the team know the effort was funded, but he didn't appreciate the approach. That ad campaign is still one of the most successful the company has ever had. For those of you who remember the little tabs you chewed as a kid to show you where to brush (and where you didn't), that was part of this campaign. They smartly included elementary education and take-home tools for dentists to give their patients. They even had a kid-friendly mascot and song. This had not been done with toothpaste before. The sales experienced double-digit growth.

If it weren't for the bravery of my Dad's colleagues and their belief in their research, this may have never happened due to what I call "me me me" syndrome.

Many articles and books have focused recently on narcissism and the "me me me" syndrome is related. What might be different here is that "me me me" sometimes only comes up at work, and the person doesn't show this as much in their "regular life".

While this can happen at the executive levels and be more noticeable there, it happens at the individual contributor level, too. Usually, it comes down to the person not liking something despite what's best for the company, customers, or employees. For whatever reason - often pride or perceived control - it's hard for the leader to let go of their beliefs. Now, let's be clear: sometimes, the executive has information not everyone does, and what doesn't make sense at the moment is the right thing to do. The difference in that - very subtle - is that it's based on data or experience - not pride or power.

Regarding pride or power, this can take on an entire corporate tone and not be isolated to a C-level position.

In the middle of my career, I was in a US-based company that had a European company purchase it. This gave me a unique perspective on what might happen the other way. Often, we hear of a US company taking over a "foreign" company and trying to apply US-centric ideas – and then being surprised they don't work so well. The reverse is also true.

As a quick aside, there's a common marketing story used here (42):

"A large multinational corporation once attempted to sell baby food in an African nation by using packaging designed for its home country market. The company's regular label showed a picture of a baby with a caption describing the kind of baby food contained in the jar. African consumers took one look at the product, however, and were horrified. They interpreted the labels to mean that the jars contained ground-up babies!"

It's not clear if this story has truth to it or it's a legend. Fact-finding sites like Snopes have claimed it's only a legend. Now, legend or not, this story reminds one that localization - knowing who is buying your product and who you are working with - is important to consider before deciding to do things the same way.

Okay, back to my merger story, which doesn't involve baby food. It does, however, involve energy. The energy grid in the US is a complex beast and different from other countries. It also has dozens of federal government entities and mandates, as well as state utility commissions to consider. Energy companies also have many layers of cybersecurity regulations to adhere to. If the company is also public, there is a whole other set of regulatory constraints. The European company buying us had none of these layers of regulation to deal with. Things were simpler in their country, and their grid worked differently. And yes, that company assumed that they could apply their approaches to the company they bought in the US. To the victor belong the spoils, right?

Being on the front lines of this and baffled by the approach, and knowing the impact, I gagged on my words for a bit. First, I was shocked that they weren't aware of these restrictions. Later, I was also shocked that you would only get a reply from a director of their company if you were also a director. If you contacted anyone higher, like a VP, you would not hear from them. There were other interesting and unpublished rules we mostly learned the hard way – usually by violating them.

While I'll spare you the details here, one of the approaches from that acquiring company would have resulted in major safety issues for our team in the field. When dealing with large amounts of electricity, safety is a big deal. Done wrong, you can energize an area that a tech is working on and end their life in a split second. Along with doing the right thing, I knew many of these crews personally and always thought about their safety when we were deploying systems and approaches. I could not let an image of one of my colleagues being put in harm's way out of my head.

The new ownership company wanted to apply a set of tools and an approach that we had not used before. That approach took away a lot of safety controls and put in place strange things that served no one on the US-based grid. For example, they wanted to force a different version of an operating system that only had error messages in their language (not English). They also wanted to downgrade a number of our systems that had high uptime and were efficient. These systems were already paid for and running. It was weird.

One day, I made perhaps what can be considered a mistake by asking "why". Now, how I did that was not the most constructive. I was cocky then. At the same time, our systems had the highest uptime and availability in the industry. We did this with a small team and much faster than expected. Yes, I was proud of those accomplishments and didn't receive alternative ideas well- especially ones destined to produce crap results (see, I am still a bit cocky about it).

After many meetings sharing this logic and being ignored, I communicated the concerns to the next level up. Some of these ideas have layers of complexity, and it is difficult to get them into simple bullet items with profit/loss, but I did my best. Yes, you guessed it, I angered executives not because my ideas and concerns weren't solid but because I dared to go against their edicts. Despite the data, insights, and experience - or the legal constraints of compliance - the culture of this company was that all executives were right, and they would not be questioned.

While that company enjoyed success, mostly because of incredible market conditions for energy, they also learned (the hard way) that they couldn't apply everything from their country without consequence. And, in time, I'm told they used many approaches we advocated for. However, it had to be their idea first. The stress of that in my work life, and a number of stressors in my personal life, led to me being let go from that organization. Along with some great content and stories, it was a gift not to be under those constraints anymore.

Now, while executives or a whole organization can drive the "me me me" pandemic, individual contributors can do this, too. Most of you probably have experienced a high-maintenance, self-centered personality in your work.

In the technical world, some specific roles are even celebrated for this. Entire staffs are assigned to "protect" them from others, given their abrasion. I had one of those people tell me once that they were the "Gainsburger" around the "medicine" for this high-maintenance prima donna techie. The reference is to put something palatable around pet medicine for them to swallow it. This techie had multiple patents for the company, would sometimes forget to shower, and had incredible forward-thinking ideas. They weren't mean, but they could be blunt. Their "Gainsburger" staff helped protect everyone who could get offended by the direct nature of this person. However, is a toxic personality medicine? In the longer-term and bigger picture, do they serve the organization in a way that is worth the cost? That's a hard one to answer and is a case-by-case basis.

Here is a more humorous "me me me" story about one of those personalities I traveled internationally with for work. We'll call her Brenda. Brenda was one of those people accustomed to ordering things not on a menu at a restaurant and expecting them to appear. I had seen her do this multiple times. Along with being embarrassed, I was taken aback at the audacity. If the server or restaurant didn't cater to this, it was not a pretty site.

We were on an international work trip once to a country whose language neither of us spoke much of. Their culture was different, and it was not US-friendly. That culture also had very different cuisine, which was somewhat frightening to us. Not to gross you out here, but to make a point, boiled water cockroaches were one of the local delicacies. There were all sorts of cultural norms there about food and politeness that were different and challenging to navigate. We were helping close a $300k deal, which was a big number at the time.

On cue, Brenda ordered something not on the menu. Because of the language barrier, three restaurant staff came to try and understand. They drew pictures and later said, "Ok, ok, ok," and went back to the kitchen. I did my best to order some rice and veggies, which the staff seemed very excited to provide. While I'm sure it was pretty awful, I attempted to order in their language, which they seemed to appreciate, too. A little bit later, our food came out. I did my best not to burst out laughing. There was a small parade of people, with the person in the front holding a bowl of something steaming. As it got closer, we noticed a can of Sprite burst open in the bowl. It was boiling on top of what looked like rice and maybe an egg.

The restaurant staff was so excited. They thought they gave Brenda exactly what she wanted. Brenda was about to send it back when I said something like, "You are eating all of that." I'm not sure what came over me, and for some reason, she listened. It could have been because we were the only white people there. It could also be that there were kids in uniforms with automatic weapons everywhere glaring at us. No matter what it was, it was quite a site to see Brenda and the boiling Sprite souffle.

Even if it's not a boiling can of Sprite, or endangering the lives of staff, or missing major financial opportunities, the "me me me" syndrome can have a massive negative impact on your organization. Whether it's a single executive, a whole culture, or just one super-toxic person, the impacts on morale, productivity, and profitability are immense.

It's just not worth it.

CHAPTER 24

Skill - Vent

"The goal of any true resistance is to affect outcomes, not just to vent. And the only way to affect outcomes and thrive in our lives is to find the eye in the hurricane and act from that place of inner strength."

— *Arianna Huffington*

Venting is perhaps the most well-known and used skill. It can also be the most misused. Unchecked and stuck in a loop, venting can lead to problem admiration and other BS-ities. However, with a few tiny guardrails, venting can also be a powerful tool to use.

The history of the word vent itself gives us some guidance about how this best can work. The etymology of the word comes from 14th century France and refers to eventer, which loosely translates to "let out, expose to air." More modern dictionary descriptions echo this meaning 700 years later, "an opening for the escape of a gas or liquid or for the relief of pressure." (43)

For a moment, let's reflect on what venting means and how it works, using a simple physical example - vent caps in food packaging. Stay with me, it will make sense in a moment. Vent caps are often used to package foods to keep them safe and fresh. As one of the biggest manufacturers, Tri-Sure, states in their descriptions - it is a major part of safe packaging:

"Venting a package can relieve overpressure caused by the gassing of the filling product (e.g., hydrogen peroxide). Venting can also relieve pressure caused by the cooling down of a drum after hot filling (e.g., high-viscosity liquids). Venting technology helps prevent unsafe stacking conditions of lightweight packages because of pressure changes caused by temperature variations." (44)

Here, both the physical world and the history of the word give us clues on how to best use venting as a skill:

One-Way: Notice that venting isn't a circular activity. The food caps don't have a recirculating function to let the venting cycle back and re-vent. The etymology of the word also refers to letting out - not keeping around. So, when we vent, the intention is to get that story and frustration out, ideally once. If this activity lasts more than a few times, we need to be honest that we're likely engaged in something else.

Short Time Near The Event: Venting happens near the time of the event. It doesn't stay bottled up in the food packaging, waiting to explode later. Whenever possible, find time to vent soon. For many, this can seem silly, and we believe that we shouldn't complain. However, it's structured as a vent, and you are doing yourself and your loved ones a favor. This is better than holding on to the angst because the gas will keep building up.

Letting Go: When you vent, the idea is to get rid of the thing and not to give it any more power. In one of the more poetically bizarre things in life, when we hold on to our anger and upset towards situations we don't like, we keep them alive. This was a major WTF moment when I realized it - my complaining and holding onto my grudge was hurting me more than the (insert your favorite expletive here) person that created the situation.

Let's add a few things that can helping venting be a tool to help with BS resilience at work:

Structure: Wherever possible, spend a few seconds with someone you are likely to vent to. Make up some quick rules. For example, you get to vent once about a specific situation. I know, it's fun to keep bringing it up and give it a life of its own. Or, at the moment, it can feel like that. Keeping a vent going on the same issue, without letting it go or taking action, will literally sink your precious life energies.

Two-Way: Ideally, you take on the role of venting and being vented to by another. This helps in several ways. It can prevent a "me me me" syndrome and allows a small and simple function - empathy and validation.

Empathy and Validation: Okay, here's the trick - you will not offer solutions to fix it. Shh. No. Stop. You will understand, from their perspective, their frustration. You don't have to agree or disagree with their take on things. You are going to validate that it makes sense to *them*. This is easy to do with words like, "Got it, when Jim Bob said that your tractor was a dumb orange color, it pissed you off." Then you follow-up with, "It makes sense that you would be pissed at Jim Bob for that."

Emergency Venting

Do you have a situation where you cannot connect with your vent buddy soon, or is it just too personal for that? Okay, the good news is that you can blurt out this word salad in a journal or just any piece of paper. Ideally, use a writing instrument like a pencil or pen and not just type it. The physical nature of this is cathartic. Also, it doesn't have to be linear or make any sense. Let your brain go for just a bit and put words all over the page. Drawings work, too.

You can put a timer on this so it doesn't go on forever - something under 10 minutes should do it. When done, realize you have given this thing some structure, and it's now outside of you. You don't need to give it any energy or attention anymore. It's time to shred and recycle it and let it go. Nicely done!

Extra credit skills

If you are looking for bonus points and extra credit, there's a simple technique you can use to let things go. There's a ton of brain science and psychology around this. We will keep it simple. When you define something bothering you, especially if it's somewhat silly in definition, you can put it in its place or let it go. When it's undefined or not addressed, it will keep pestering you.

Now, you might think I'm full of it (often I am), and this is absurd. But is it worth trying a few times if it works? Here's an easy way to structure a vent to let it go. This happens after the vent (remember you can write it out if you don't have a person handy to receive said vent). You may need to repeat this a few times, or it may work one time.

Remember, the more action and silliness you can engage here, the better.

Here are the steps:

1. Think of the thing you are venting about as a cloud, about the size of a soccer ball.
2. Notice the shape you give the cloud.
3. As you see this cloud, give it colors.
4. Notice the cloud's shape again. It can be any shape you want it to be. It can also change shapes if you want it to.
5. Now, give the cloud some noises. These can be silly, vulgar, or just everyday sounds. It's your cloud.
6. Give your cloud motion - is it smooth and flowy, or bumpy, or something else?
7. If you notice an attachment to the cloud and fear comes up from letting it go, let yourself know you'll be okay. It doesn't need to hang around anymore.
8. Give the cloud a path, say from left to right in front of you. Have it make its sounds, shapes, colors, and motions as it goes along its cloud path.
9. Imagine the cloud, with the colors, shape, sound and movement, going from the far-left side to the far-right side, in front of you.
10. After it's outside of your field of vision, it's gone.
11. You may need to repeat this a couple of times or over a couple of days.

Now, if this feels absurd or "woo woo" to you, you aren't alone. The first few times I tried it, I had serious self-questioning. WTF am

I doing? However, every time I've done this, the thing - or at least a big part of it - goes away. I've used this same coping mechanism with family, friends, and co-workers, and it's had the same results.

And, if this cloud exercise doesn't work for you, that's okay, too. Venting is just one tool, and there are many others to choose from to help with building up their BS Resilience.

"Some people can vent their anger, take a breath, and let it go, but I wasn't one of them." - Paul Allen

Everyone has a mix of tools that help them move forward. Some tools also work in specific situations, and other tools may only be needed later. It's sort of like foods we might have hated as a kid, but we later grow to like them. What's awesome too, maybe like what our mom's may have said to us with food, is that trying a new skill will not kill us.

CHAPTER 25

BS Issue - Shiny Object Syndrome

"You can always find a distraction if you're looking for one."

— *Tom Kite*

With Shiny Object Syndrome (SOS), the pattern goes something like this:

1. Teams are working on a hard problem that is more difficult than they thought. The effort might require hard decisions about staffing or tough realizations about the value the company is or isn't doing. There may be some challenging technical work, or it may shine a bright light on some decisions that don't make sense anymore. It's probably not defined as easy.

2. Almost unconsciously, using the coping mechanism of distraction, people may cling to a new thing with SOS. Let's call it Doodely-Cha-Cha (DCC). At a recent conference, someone learned that DCC fixes everything, and it's fun and easy. There are shiny diagrams, great videos, and the people are really nice. They showed another company with the same issue getting great results with DCC.

3. DCC shows up on the scene with a needs assessment engagement that shows where things are compared to peers and how DCC can uniquely fix everything. Everyone gets

excited, and somehow, funding is created for this new critical effort - DCC.

4. If someone is brave enough to say, "Why DCC?" they are often labeled as luddites or not wanting to see the company succeed. If they bring up the hard problems that have not been solved by DCC, they are ignored.

Most often, SOS solutions like DCC do not entirely do what they claim. This is often due to how the company uses them or the DCC tools themselves. And, about 12-18 months later, the company finds they are in the same (or worse) situation and are somewhat surprised that their choices led them back.

Small and Fast

SOS doesn't have to only exist in big hairy situations. We can find it with small and fast things, too. While we all love quick fixes and acting, sometimes this approach, combined with SOS, can be especially disastrous.

At a previous company, the central corporate office was struggling to communicate with the field sales organization. The field sales folks shared they didn't have the best tools to work with clients. The products they sold were complex, and showing a client's information working with the right products was a powerful sales tool.

This company was slow to act and risk-averse. Their industry was this way by design. So, some of that slowness was a good thing. However, some of it was a corporate culture that attacked any change and new ideas violently. As you might imagine, the field executives and central office executives clashed over many things.

Field executives were connected to their customers and what they could and couldn't sell. Central office executives were connected to mandates and regulations that could put them out of business if not adhered to.

One day, just before a large field event, the top field executive bought his 500 staff new iPads. This would fix everything and let them show customers their products more easily when they are in the field. He made many promises during the event, and the field sales team was super excited.

Because of the friction, this field executive didn't tell the central executives about this. They just did it. Just giving out iPads doesn't make all the company applications usable. Also, this company had some serious privacy and security Federal and State mandates to adhere to for its data. Securing this data in devices like iPads was in its infancy and not entirely possible.

While the intent may have been awesome - enabling field teams to do their job more easily and giving them tools - the result was disastrous. Those iPads didn't work with the corporate systems and became useless for work. The field teams let their kids play games on them and used them for social media.

And, while this did get the central organization more in gear, they took nearly four years to roll out secure, useful applications and access. By then, those iPads were at the end of life and new devices had to be deployed.

SOS Can Look Smart

One of the more dangerous SOS approaches can disguise itself as something smart to do. I see this a lot in technology, where very smart vendors and industries create what looks like new patterns. One technical area where this occurs often is in application integration patterns.

Keeping it simple here, integration between computer systems is batch (done once or a few times a day) or event-based (done in near real-time, usually near an event). A simple example of batch can include syncing-up all the financial transactions on a daily, weekly, monthly, or quarterly basis. Often, it makes sense to do this once/day instead of every financial transaction in real-time. Different in approach, an example of an event-based transaction would be when you buy something online, and dozens of integrations inform credit card systems to charge your account, fulfillment systems to package and ship your thing, and email systems to send you information.

For event-based integration systems, it's common to use APIs - Application Programming Interfaces. Now, there are a lot of nuances here, and if this book had comments, I'd have lots of smart people telling me how wrong I am about little nuances. I'm keeping this simple to make a point and not provide details. Sorry, tech friends. It'll be okay. You can vent or smash if you need to.

All right, well, if we believe vendors, there are massive differences between API approaches, and we need to change them every few years to a new thing. We are told this new thing will make a big difference. Many vendors will get into some interesting nuances of how to use these messages and the applications they talk to, with a scheme that makes the integration somehow more efficient.

What's interesting - based on thousands of deployments I've led and seen and many vendors I've talked to - is that what is packaged up in those slow, old batch systems is used as payload in their event-based APIs. They are still sending the equivalent of digital paper. It's faster, and closer to the event, and has many advantages. But really, it's just more digital paper.

And, while there are some amazing integration patterns like publish-subscribe, they are used much less than one would hope. For example, this publish-subscribe pattern would let many systems subscribe to a single new message. One good example here would be an address change for a customer. When this change happens, many systems likely need to be updated with this information. Instead of writing and maintaining dozens of integrations, you can have a single publish-subscribe setup. When new systems come along, they subscribe to this message.

As much as we love to think we're being innovative with integrations with novel and new ideas, looking at the history tells a different story and is almost humorous (45):

- 1945 – An early computer called EDSAC had a library catalog of how to use subroutines in a program on paper tape. (46)
- 1957 - First API specification noted as a concept in the book *The Preparation of Programs for an Electronic Digital Computer* (47)
- 1968 - APIs are described interfacing computers with graphics cards in several conferences (48)
- 1971 - FTP (file transfer protocol), commonly used to transport data, is created at MIT (49)

- 1974 - APIs are applied to database work (50)
- 1990 - Web APIs are created along and see usage in languages like Java
- 1998 - Service Oriented Architectures are introduced along with the SOAP protocol (51)
- 2000 - API protocols mature with the REST and the RESTful approach (52)
- 2005 – Microservices are formally introduced by Peter Rodgers (53), while there seems to be activity here as early as 1999

So, depending on when you are reading this and how you like to interpret something starting, this "new" integration technology being talked about by the latest SOS may be 83 years old or 19 years young. In either case, it's not new. Let's be clear: it's important to stay current with technologies and platforms and avoid technical debt. However, the new things are rarely as new as purported.

This pattern is not unique to technology. SOS is often used when a corporate culture or key personalities make it difficult to move forward. Or, if the problems feel large and the company doesn't want to deal with them, then. In these cases, you'll see a lot of SOS.

The mantras behind them will either be to centralize ("think of all the money we'll save if we do things the same way and we'll avoid duplicate efforts") or to decentralize ("put the tools with the people who love it and think how fast we can go now"). The right mix of these two – a hybrid approach - usually works out to be the best solution. Often this can be done without SOS - no matter what whitepaper your awesome vendor shares… or how nice they are.

CHAPTER 26

Skill - Shiny Object Syndrome

"A déjà vu is usually a glitch in the Matrix. It happens when they change something."

— *Trinity in the movie The Matrix*

Wait, what? SOS is a skill, too? I thought it was BS!?

Yes, you just read about how Shiny Object Syndrome can be a BS at work thing. Poetically, it can be a positive skill you can leverage. For those of you who are parents, you may have used this with your toddlers. When they throw a tantrum or get super stuck in something, you might have used a bright shiny toy or a snack, to get them unstuck.

Similarly, at work, we may know someone who can get stuck in their story. In daily status meetings, they can find something to complain about - maybe the same thing - and expound on this noise, filling the space with dread. Their RAS has this "hit" on high rotation, and they are sharing it with everyone else. While a shiny object won't fix their issues, the distraction may break up the greatest hits parade enough that the misery stops for a time - for everyone. Examples of shiny objects here you can use might be new topics, something happy everyone can agree upon, and the equivalent of "look a squirrel!" When using shiny objects, do your best to pick something at least moderately positive. For example, a negative news story will just spread more doom and gloom. However, a positive story might interrupt things enough for the greatest hits to stop.

Scary Sam in the Stand-Up Meetings

It was Sam's turn in the daily stand-up. The rules were to share what you were working on that day and if you had any blockers or issues you needed help with. Outside of that stand-up, someone on the team would sync-up with you on whatever was needed. This is a major tenant of the agile process and is used in most technical teams as part of development. In person, it's often literally done standing up in a circle, which helps things move fast and helps people stay focused. These meetings are generally very brief.

Everyone would noticeably brace when Sam would start. We knew the same old complaint would come up again. We were tired of this and had no empathy reserves left. He also didn't seem to do that much work, and we were bored of listening to his top hits.

"Today, I'm trying to edit the file and update my script. Nobody seems to read this, and I get a lot of calls for it because they aren't reading it. If they only read it, they wouldn't need to call me." whined Sam.

Now, Sam's documentation online was some of the ugliest ever. It was hard to read. And, by "a lot" of phone calls that Sam described, it was actually one or two calls a week. People actually didn't call Sam because they didn't want to hear him complain. However, they were stuck and needed help. At the same time, Scott's peers were doing relatively huge things daily while he stayed stuck in a traffic jam in Whinesville, population one.

Ideally, some intervention from leadership should take place here. Sam was a drain on a high-performing team and became more annoying. However, the leader was asleep at the wheel or not sure what to do - or both. So, it fell on a peer on the team to do something... or to accept that the greatest hits would play.

Here with Sam, many had offered to help with edits, graphics and other things to make his documentation more useful to others. He refused, mostly because he thought his documentation was the most accurate and "right". More of the greatest hits from Sam.

One day, I got brave and asked Sam for help with a project. I didn't need it, and I didn't look forward to him whining, but I thought I should try something. He was honestly smart and talented technically. Socially, however, it was a different story. I had some work that needed technical details that I didn't yet know how to solve. I freely admitted that it wasn't done yet and needed his expertise.

To my surprise, he jumped right in. He seemed excited to help. Okay, it was a bit weird at first, and the greatest hits (whining) continued some. He also was a little bit condescending at first, which I chose to suck up. It didn't continue for long, so I didn't need to put the smack down. Then I noticed something: Sam was scared to death. He was intimidated that his skills might not be needed anymore, and he didn't have much new to work on. Scott was older than some techs on the team, and things were changing fast. Now, Sam and I will never be best friends. We would annoy the heck out of each other too much. However, he made my work product worlds better. The next day at stand-up, he had something new to talk about. And he didn't complain. We were all in a bit of shock.

About a week later, Sam came to me with an idea he was excited about. Scott was a senior engineer, and I had just started. Something clicked for him that some people didn't understand - not because they were lazy - but because they didn't learn by reading like he did. Yes, that's a big "duh" to many of us- but this was an epiphany for Sam. Sam knew I was okay with graphical interfaces and had a little experience with learning modalities. I was also closer to the demographic he was trying to help. In what seemed a more bizarre twist, Sam asked for my help. He wanted his documentation to have a little navigation and be easier for others to read. Now, he didn't love that he had to change what was "right," but he seemed to understand that this would help others. We worked on this together. In days, Sam had dozens, then hundreds of more hits on his web pages. Soon after that, he was asked for help on a few key projects closer to what he specialized in.

And yes, we still heard some of his greatest hits in our daily standup, but they were in less rotation, and we heard a lot more about progress on things. He even asked for help.

All it took for change here was a bit of a shiny object. And yes, it took swallowing my pride and dislike for about 30 minutes. However, it was worth it to interrupt the droning pattern of whining about nothing.

Five Steps to Use SOS

To have tools at the ready, here are five ideas to use Shiny Object Syndrome to interrupt a pattern of poo:

1. Think of something positive, not related, that you can bring up.

2. Be ready for small results first. They may say something like, "Yeah, that's cool, but whine, complain, whine."

3. Be ready to follow up with the positive and even ask for their help with something.

4. Crank up your tolerance. The first interactions might be rough.

5. Be open to their input in helping your work product.

Along with peers, SOS can be used with managers and senior leaders. You can use the same tools that pro marketers use to have companies invest millions in their solutions. Pay attention to what this leader focuses on. Is there anything they repeat? Is there a way you can echo one of those things and incorporate it with a shiny new object? Is there a project or solution you want them to consider? See if you can weave that in. Some execs honestly love nothing more than to hear themselves talk. As BS as that can be, use it to your advantage. Paraphrase what they say a lot of and weave it into some new action you want. As annoying as this might be, and you may even feel like you are dumbing yourself down, go for the result. A small amount of this may tweak things, so you enjoy your workplace that much more.

SOS Can Work Small Miracles

After hearing what felt like a lecture and repeated monologue for the millionth time from my leader, Barbara, I knew I would snap if I heard it again. What she was talking about was what we were already ten steps ahead of. Her style was demeaning. She thought she was the smartest person ever. Even if she was, this was a crappy way to treat people. She was not honestly aware of her "me me me" syndrome.

One day, I'm not sure what came over me, but instead of cringing and running away quickly, I used one of her mantras and then did an SOS. While I don't remember the exact details, as it was honestly some random moment, I somehow wove something I wanted to do with something Barbara liked. To my surprise, she acknowledged it and said that it was a good idea and let me run with it. In relatively short order, I was promoted to a leadership role in her organization. She gave me free rein to do a few things others didn't seem to have the freedom to do. She even let me build up a team and work on products that didn't totally align with her beliefs. Now, she still could be demeaning and have her mantras, but the volume of those turned down. And, instead of bearing them (and complaining too much later), I used them to my advantage.

Years later, Barbara gave me some of the best recommendations I have had in my career. And, in some dire life circumstances, it helped me find lucrative work quickly. Sometimes, the annoying people (to us) can become our greatest allies, and all it takes is a little bit of a shiny object syndrome to get there.

CHAPTER 27

BS Issue - Wrongful Accusation

"Accusation reveals the character of the accuser more than the accused"

— *Bangambiki Habyarimana*

If you work and live long enough, it's likely that you'll be accused of something you didn't do. For some of you, this can be a daily occurrence based on how you were born. For others, this is a rarer occurrence. Regardless, receiving this prejudice can be shocking and make you furious. For those who care deeply about being productive, effective and aware - most likely you because you are reading this book - being accused of the opposite can be appalling. It's easy, in this state, to second-guess and wonder what you may have done wrong. And, while some self-reflection is always good, be careful you don't fall into a guilt complex.

According to WebMD, "Excessive guilt, however, is when guilt turns sour. It can lead to anxious obsessions, depressive tendencies, and physical symptoms if it's not addressed." (54)

Navigating Wrongful Accusations

We had a tight timeline to produce results for a senior executive. He was looking for some prototypes and new insights for a few projects. He wasn't sure our current insights and beliefs were well-founded and was concerned the actions we took might not be effective. While not continuous, he wanted different perspectives offered, backed by insights and data.

My team had new tools to quickly visualize complex data, and a strong team skilled at this approach. It was common practice for us to do many prototypes and data visualizations in these situations, usually in a few days. Some of these data visualizations lived on to be used in an ongoing way and were used daily. Others had a short lifespan once the issue was better understood. The team members and team were praised for their strength here and often called "rock stars".

After putting two of my more skilled data pros on this new effort and request by our executive, I was fairly stunned by their response. They wanted to do exactly what our executive asked us *not* to do, which was to consult the existing teams. Those existing teams had a number of beliefs and ideas that didn't seem to align with the data, and so our executive wanted an alternative look at things. Also, this specific effort had a known short lifespan. It was like many similar projects we did, and it was not unusual for this to be the case. The visualization work was not throw-away and helped the company move forward, but might not be looked at every day. The team understood this was not a reflection of their work and that it helped the company decide things rapidly. And finally, we all knew that our visualizations had errors and were not perfect. They were directionally correct, but the rapid delivery time did not let us address all aspects of the analysis, and there were variances because of this. The data pros were given great leeway here.

For whatever reason, this new assignment was incredibly disruptive to these two individuals, and their resistance was unusual.

Soon, I heard rumors I was being accused of many things that were inaccurate or not my intent. Those accusations were things I worked hard to make sure were not issues. However imperfect I was as a leader, my intents and actions didn't line up with what I was being accused of.

During this time, we had several meetings with senior executives that were incredibly intense. It was unpleasant. However, because of the accusations, I needed to stay calm and focused. I made the mistake of sharing with my executive that I wasn't sure what I was being accused of but heard the rumors. I explained my approach and my history as a leader championing people and being an advocate.

His response was not what I expected. He quoted Hamlet - "The lady doth protest too much, methinks." My interpretation of this was him telling me I was guilty of whatever this thing was. To this day, I still don't have clarity on this thing. However, HR interviewed me, again with no details, and told there was an investigation. Of what this was about, they couldn't say. In my entire career, I've never had this, so it was scary and frustrating. Keeping my wits about me and not letting this get to me was challenging.

At the same time, I have had friends and colleagues experience what I was being falsely accused of. Sadly, that pattern can happen in the workplace more often than not - and is often unchecked. So, while I understood the pattern, I knew I wasn't part of it. And, at the same time, I brutally and constantly second-guessed my every action - "Did I somehow do this?" and "What could I have done that was close to this?"

Despite all this mess, the team delivered a few useful insights that helped the company make different decisions. Still, every day was painful. The passive-aggressive behavior and quiet accusations didn't stop. It started to affect the team, and I could tell they were unsure what was going on. While I had others on the team experience me as an ally and champion, these two had a different experience. However, because of the delicate nature of this, I was told I could not just work things out directly. Walking around an office, being looked at, and pre-judged for being something that I didn't do was awful. I wanted to scream "I didn't do anything wrong" - but that would create suspicion, like it did with the executive I mentioned. It also made me angry because I couldn't think of anything to do about this.

This situation gave me a super tiny glimpse of what prejudice feels like on the receiving end. That was especially stunning. I was imagining what it is like to be called lazy if you are a certain race, or a criminal if you are another race - by a prejudiced bigot. Holy (expletive), that's awful - and living something mildly similar for a short time gave me a tiny understanding of that world.

To this day, I still don't have clarity on what the issue was. Those two individuals did later apply for and accept jobs in different parts of the company. What they probably don't know is the amazing positive reviews I gave their new leaders to help that along. I highlighted what they were great at and said little else. I hope that they let go of whatever was vexing them, and they continued to be recognized for their great parts of work. Later, when they left the company for another, I also received reference calls from those companies and gave positive reviews for the good parts of their work.

And yes, the HR investigation apparently ended. Although, those things are unclear and secretive and keep the alleged violator in a state of wondering what happened. It took several years for that wrongful accusation and perception to leave my brain space. Writing this still brings up strong emotions for me. My teams have been successful and win multiple industry awards. Similar accusations by others never occurred again - even with the likely oversight of HR "watching".

So, what do you do if this happens to you?

While I don't wish this drama and stress on anyone, here's what I wish I had done more of:

Get crazy calm, at least at work. Outside of work, vent and seek help, but at work, get calmer than you ever have before. Become like a Zen Monk if the noise gets louder. This doesn't make it right what they did, but calm will win. Do your best not to talk about it. That will be hard. Focus on your work product, dates, and deliverables. Remember to compliment achievements by anyone who has them.

Document everything. In a private journal or digital document you own (not a company document or on their systems), write down times, dates, events and people involved. Hopefully, you will never need this. However, there's nothing like a list like this to use if you are questioned. You don't have to share it, but perhaps you have detailed records of the events if asked. You may also want to download or print-out any company guidelines or codes of conduct to have handy.

Refrain from second-guessing. Allow yourself one or two rounds of "what could I have done differently" or "how did they perceive it". Then, stop. Doing this continually will have you take on a guilt complex. In this example, I spiraled out of control, feeling like shit here. Don't do that.

Apologize only if you need to. Now, if you find something concrete, apologize publicly for that specific issue. It can be simple, "Hey, I wanted to say I'm sorry. Reflecting on events, I could see how when I said X, it seemed like Y. It makes sense that one might perceive this, even though that is not my intent. I am sorry for any issues this may have caused." Be careful not to over-apologize.

Realize some people love drama. Some people will spin, start rumors, and make up crap. It's not fun, and it's about them creating more BS "greatest hits" for themselves. Ignore it. If you can get there, laugh about it to yourself.

Do something for yourself. There will be more stress and drama for a time. This is a good time to get a massage, hit the hot tub, and let go in the healthiest ways you know how to. Drinking more is not on the list here, although that might be tempting.

Use the "smash" tool here. If done right and in private, this might help a lot.

Talk to a lawyer. While I hope you don't have to take legal action to protect yourself, knowing your options here can be helpful. Don't flaunt this, as it will put the company on the defensive. However, having that list of facts and events mentioned above for your lawyer to review will help them quickly assess your rights and ideas for any next steps.

To be clear: if someone does do something at work that needs to go to your leaders and/or HR, report it. This is important. Many injustices in many workplaces should be reported and aren't. And, if you hear someone is accused of something at work, do your best not to assume immediate guilt. The situation is probably a lot more complicated than you realize. It's not like that movie or TV show – it's a lot harder. All parties involved will experience considerable trauma.

CHAPTER 28

Skill - This is It

As far as we know, this is the only present moment we will get.

This is it.

This is our chance to choose action - or not.

This is our moment to rise above - or stay stuck in the quagmire.

This is our time to do something new - or to keep saying "someday".

This is the only moment that we will have *this* moment.

Yes, there are all sorts of circumstances that can make life hard. How we were born, where we were born, how tired we are, how hard we work, what's going on in our families, what our friends said, what our loved-ones said, what hasn't shown up yet, we're scared, what our boss did, we're angry, what has shown up so far, how much debt we have, how little we make, how we can't see a future, how we deserve more, how we are doomed, etc.

Despite those circumstances and beliefs, this is it.

This is our moment.

It's gone now.

Now, this is our next moment.

What do you want to do with these precious moments?

What are you worth?

What step will you take right now?

This is it.

I have many thanks for the teachings of "This is It". It's been powerful in my life for decades now. These teachings come from a program called SuperCamp by Quantum Learning. I was fortunate enough to go to that program in my teens, later be a counselor there and work for their corporate offices for a time. Their programs continue to this day, and I highly recommend checking them out. (29)

One of their tenants is called the "8 Keys to Success". This is one of those keys and their program does a phenomenal job explaining this and how to use it. Forty years after learning this, I still use this approach nearly every week.

Life is short and precious. This is it.

CHAPTER 29

BS Issue - Yes-people and Brown-nosers

> *"Flattery feeds directly into our ego and our self-identity. It makes us feel good about ourselves, so naturally, we are not immune to its charms. In fact, flattery affects behavior outside of our awareness. We have a tendency to respond more positively to situations, people, and products that make us feel good about ourselves."*
>
> *– Dr. AJ Marsen*

Ah, the yes-people and brown-nosers. It's a bit crazy that in these modern times, they still exist and thrive. They have yet to go extinct. Before we jump into a story about how this BS issue still proliferates in modern workplaces, let's look at the brain science here for some clues.

Now, most of us would like to think of ourselves as rational decision-makers - weighing the pros and cons of a situation and using insights from data to make decisions, right? Well, we aren't entirely set up to do that. We are not plumbed that way. While we do have parts of our "rational" brain in our prefrontal cortex involved in decision-making, we also have some relatively ancient environments heavily involved in our brain. These are in our limbic system, including the amygdala. Experts share that "the amygdala is especially important for decision-making, by triggering autonomic responses to emotional stimuli, including monetary reward and punishment." (55) What's clear in this research is that when the amygdala does not develop completely or is damaged, people struggle greatly with decision making. What's also interesting is that language, reason and logic don't exist in the limbic system. Now, this is greatly over-simplified to the brain scientists reading this (and maybe also the aliens). However, science shows that most of our decisions are heavily emotionally based.

So, how does that relate to brown-nosing and yes-people? Well, say you are a leader and perhaps have a fragile self-worth. With someone saying how great they think you are, your amygdala will probably respond favorably to this person. Over time, that person may enjoy more accolades. If that person is also in sync with their leader's RAS greatest hits (what they complain about and talk about a lot), that leader will probably also be more favorable to this person. Now, in and of themselves, these things aren't that awful. Leaders have hard jobs and need first followers to move things along. Further, not having to discuss every decision can be a relief, given the massive volume of decisions at hand. However, when the world changes, as it does more frequently, it takes different decisions, information, and greatest hits for the organization to adapt and succeed. If the brown-noser and yes-person culture is out of check, it's a matter of time before a large failure occurs.

Cheerleading Gone Wrong

"Wow, that was such a great presentation. I loved how you connected the graphic of the cube with the work we are doing." emoted a co-worker. She was brilliant in her own right but had clearly learned to compliment (and often over-compliment) her leader. Most of the rest of us threw up a little bit in our mouths when we heard this. We'll call her Tina and our boss Frank.

Frank missed this over-done compliment or didn't care and seemed to gloat about how great he thought he was. He said something of the sort. There was more quiet hurling by the team. Frank was smart, but the presentation wasn't earth-shattering. It was helpful. It was good. But the amount of praise Tina gave was so overdone that it cheapened the good parts about Frank's presentation. To be fair, Tina was probably on autopilot with her praise. She was in a mostly male environment and had to do a lot of things to validate her worth. That pattern also makes me hurl. Tina was strong at bringing complex ideas together. She was great at getting prima donnas to create value and to stop grooming themselves. Tina also had many creative ideas she seemed afraid to share. However, the amount of brown-nosing she did for Frank made me not want to have anything to do with her.

Sports Analogies Overdone

Let's be clear, though, that this isn't just a female-male thing in the workplace, and there can be a massive amount of "good old boys" syndrome at play. Here is an example of just that.

"Let's centralize how we do everything with a common playbook" shared the new CIO. About seven bobble-heads started nodding. I noticed they dressed almost the same as the CIO – khakis and shirts from Eddie Bauer. These were people with 20 years' experience and advanced degrees. However, they somehow dumbed themselves down and became yes-men instantly.

The CIO, we'll call Walter, loved sports analogies. He wanted us to have plays we called (or that he called) as part of our way of doing things. As part of doing this, he had part of his team launch some of the ugliest internal web pages I have ever seen. This is where we were all to share our "plays". It was expected that we could simplify some very complex technical and software development concepts into plays that could be executed in a few seconds. Now, some of this worked for things in infrastructure. There were plays to help ensure we had high uptime and checklists to handle things when they went south. In that case, many of these concepts worked. However, there was a deaf ear for the many places they didn't apply.

Part of my team was doing some heavy research and development on new security methodologies. My co-workers were scary smart people, and I'm honestly not sure how I got grouped with them to this day. Many hold patents, have discovered the latest prime numbers, created new protocols and other feats of technical brilliance. While maybe they could be more held accountable for outcomes and milestones, simplifying this sort of research and experimentation to a football play just didn't make sense. While our boss at the time tried to protect us from the corporate offensive coordinator and assistant coaches (yes, they used those terms, too), he couldn't do that completely. I'm almost surprised that we didn't get jerseys and players' cards - that's how far he was taking things.

I remember a meeting where the yes-men were adamant that some of our research on new security methodologies should have plays and touchdowns. For context, this work was the equivalent of modern blockchain technology, but 20 years before it was introduced. The assistant coaches missed some of the subtle humor of the team. They yes-men also made up some things without anything to do with the R&D success but that they could keep score on. It was somewhat humorous because the crazy, smart, and rebellious engineers found a way for our team to get the highest score. This confused the assistant coaches and yes-men, as they clearly wanted to "get" these R&D people who didn't seem to play ball with their way of thinking.

I was scared to death of countering the CIO (head coach) with new ideas. I was new in my career and needed my job. Student loan payments were high, as was the cost of living where I worked then. But that fear was not unique to me, and many brilliant people became players for this CIO out of fear of being cut from the team. One day I somehow got the courage (or audacity) to find time to chat with him. To his credit, he made 15 minutes for me and was nice. I practiced my one question and started it off with kind words and giving him an out if he needed it. My question went something like, "Walter, we don't live our entire real-world lives at a football game. We do other things the rest of that day and the rest of that week. Do you think some things outside of football should be involved with that playbook?"

Walter stopped for a second. I could tell he thought about what I said. He looked a little puzzled, then a little angry. He was probably confused that I wasn't just going along with his "great" coaching and what he thought were novel ideas. He asked for an example, which I had prepared and shared. It was a solid one and hard to take apart. He stopped again, mentioned he had a next appointment (nobody was waiting) and that his team would get back to me. Later, I emailed him to thank him for his time. I never heard about this again, from him or any of his coaching staff. Well, that's not entirely true. In my next review, there was an anonymous comment by "leadership" that I was "not always a team player". This countered everything else in my review, and I knew where it came from. Thanks, coach!

Five Tips to Cope

Now, BS like this will exist in many workplaces, whether it's as absurd as what I depicted or something more subtle. And, some appropriate appreciation of good work, and reasonable support of our leaders is healthy. Being in constant conflict or disagreement helps no one.

Luckily, the experts in this space have guidance I wish I knew more about with Walter and team (56):

Agree with the brown-noser where you can: Without becoming a brown-noser of the brown-noser yourself, you can help. Experts say this "may decrease their need for constant approval from the boss and give them reassurances that they are a necessary part of the team."

Compliment the brown-noser: Try something like "You're pretty great at that yourself! And I love the work that Sally and Bob did on this, too."

Recognize The Noser of Brown: They may honestly not get many compliments or have a strong self-worth. So, where you can, recognize them for the good things they have done. Experts suggest something like "Taylor really helped me out last week getting all our walk-in clients seen. I really appreciate her initiative and professionalism."

Share Recognition Where You Can: While this can be tough if you put most of the work effort. However, you know what you have done (and so does everyone else). So, where you can, share complements and direct praise for coworkers. This could sound like "Brian handled key parts of that project. He's the one who deserves the compliment."

Private Quick Chat: If you have a decent relationship with the brown-noser, have a quick casual chat with them when you can. You can say something like "Hey it seems like you want to stay in Walter's good graces. I know he already thinks highly of you and your work on that project. We all do."

Remember, as annoying as yes-people and brown-nosers are, many are simply on autopilot. So instead of letting them fall asleep at the wheel, you can help them. It's a lot better outcome than floating down the work cesspool with them.

CHAPTER 30

Skill - Meditation and Visualization

> *"Take your passion (what a feeling) and make it happen (being's believing)"*
>
> — *Flashdance (What A Feeling)*

While it's more mainstream now and common for top executives and athletes to do it, many still shun visualization and mediation as being too "woo-woo". They don't realize that they are already doing it (or something close), but just not yet in a way that benefits them yet. For example, when sitting in traffic, do you sometimes stew over the cars in front of you? Do you curse out (out loud or just in your brain) that driver that cut you off or didn't signal? I know I do, even on my best days.

Or, when we think of our commutes, to use the same example, do we envision them going smoothly, or do we fear them and paint a picture of angst, stress and overwhelm? Most of us imagine the worst and dread our commutes as a mind-numbing part of the day. For those of you that don't commute, you likely have something else. Maybe it's that one meeting that brings up dread. We may dread a specific person, client, or situation we have decided will go poorly.

Guess what? You are using the same principles of visualization and even meditation in these circumstances and may be literally asking for bad outcomes. So, why not make a few small tweaks and use your powers for good?

"Be not the slave of your own past - plunge into the sublime seas, dive deep, and swim far, so you shall come back with new self-respect, with new power, and with an advanced experience that shall explain and overlook the old."

— **Ralph Waldo Emerson**

When I realized that I was already visualizing and meditating, it made using this skill much easier. What's also rad is that it wasn't required that I don an orange robe, go to a mountain top, and shave my head. A few simple tweaks in my routine made a big difference. Let's first look at the science and evidence behind visualization and meditation.

According to the experts here, "Studies have shown that visualization can help enhance cognitive processes such as attention, concentration, and memory. Visualization has also been found to be effective in reducing stress and anxiety levels." (57) But when we imagine a threat, it can create the same body chemistry of experiencing that threat directly. A study published in Neuron goes further to suggest that "Visualizing the scenario of succeeding in a difficult situation or achieving your goals can activate the same areas in your brain as physically experiencing this scenario. This promotes neuroplasticity - the formation and strengthening of the pathways in your brain related to your success - and in turn, reduces your stress, makes you more likely to succeed, and gives you a surge of motivation." (58)

A highly cited study at the University of Windsor found a reduction in stress and anxiety levels for surgeons and police officers who used visualization. Over 10 weeks, they found that subjects using visualization experience "better problem-based coping, less sleep difficulties, and reduced stomach issues." (59)

Visualization has been used in sports for some time, from Bruce Lee to Muhammad Ali. Along the hundreds of examples, "Michael Phelps' coach also talked about how he swims the race hundreds of times in his head before he actually does it. By rehearsing mentally, he becomes calm and ready to perform at his best." (60)

Even more interesting, and maybe even more out there, is that muscle strength can increase with visualization alone. Some new studies have found that physical strength went up as much as 35% *without physical exercises* and with focused visualization (61).

So, given all this evidence, maybe, just maybe, visualization might help with some BS situations at your work. The approach can be simple. Although relatively easy to start, you might at first struggle to visualize more positive outcomes. Be open to the possibility that positive outcomes could occur.

Find a few moments in your day and allow yourself to imagine in a big way. You can tell your negative filters (and yes, those top hits your RAS is playing) to take a break for a bit. Pick a specific issue or situation you would like to be different.

1. Slow down your breathing - five to ten deep breaths are usually enough. This will help create calm and get your prefrontal cortex ready to work for you.

2. Write down what you want. No filters here. What do you want the outcome or situation to be? Literally write it down and/or draw it.

3. Close your eyes and imagine yourself in an epic movie or TV show where this new vision is coming true. Connect with how it feels. What is that emotion? How do you feel relieved or elated? Note the colors and sounds around you. The more you can engage all your senses in this, the better. Stay with this for a few minutes.

4. Imagine a pathway to this destination. What's a small first step you can take towards it? When can you take that step? See yourself doing it.

5. As you come out of that visualization, jot down a few notes. If you made a next step idea, schedule that action on your calendar for some time in the next 7 days.

6. Schedule your next 10-minute visualization in the next 24 hours. You are at least as important as everything else on that calendar.

If you are like me, sometimes it is rough to see the outcome. You have hundreds and maybe thousands of pieces of information that work sucks, work is BS, and there's nothing you can do about it. It will take more than a few visualizations to change that. It took weeks, and maybe years, to create these stories. So, for the first few visualizations, you may need to go with something like, "I don't know how, but I'm open to the possibility of this changing." Yes, this might sound lame and crunchy groovy to many. Remember, there's science and a boatload of evidence around visualization working for all sorts of people.

Results may come quickly, or they may come in fits and starts and may take a little bit to present themselves as you do this work. Plan on doing this daily, for around five weeks, for shifts to start. While you are doing this, you are also entering a light-guided meditation state, so you are effectively doing two positive health practices at once. Nicely done!

This skill pairs well with many others. One of my favorites is pairing it with the wonderment process. After visualizing, we are more receptive to different approaches and ideas and may see things we didn't when our mindset was locked and we believed we were doomed. These are subtle and lead to minor course corrections that make a big difference.

One story that relates to this is one of my favorites about tankers. Yes, those giant ships that carry tons of cargo all over the world, with their multi-color metal boxes that cranes load and unload in ports. Because of their mass, they stop their engines 15 miles before they need to stop. While they have a "crash stop" routine for emergencies, this takes 15 minutes to execute. Imagine for a moment that you had to perform an emergency stop on your commute and that it took 15 minutes. You would probably have to collide with many things as this occurred. Yeah, that would be a mess.

Because of the ship's massive weight and how fluid dynamics work, turning has a similar issue for these large ships. As it turns out (pun intended), if you just attempt to move the rudder to steer these ships while underway, the force required is phenomenal and slow.

You could break the rudder. However, modern supertankers have a trim tab. This is a small piece of metal on the end of the rudder. It makes a focused effort to move a little bit. In doing so, it creates less resistance for the rudder to move and then the giant ship to move.

The analogy here is that our beliefs about work being BS is the giant tanker. We can rarely stop them quickly and may tend to crash when we try. To steer a different course, say somewhere else than "work sucks and is BS," we need a little focused effort. Our trim tabs are skills like visualization. They create the space for the potential for us to steer to a different outcome.

While I've heard this story many times, I didn't realize that it comes from Buckminster Fuller, the famous inventor and philosopher. He was also in the US Navy in World War I, and he shared it in a magazine article in 1972 (62):

> "Something hit me very hard once, thinking about what one little man could do. Think of the Queen Elizabeth — the whole ship goes by and then comes the rudder. And there's a tiny thing at the edge of the rudder called a trim tab. It's a miniature rudder. Just moving the little trim tab builds a low pressure that pulls the rudder around. Takes almost no effort at all. So, I said that the little individual can be a trim tab. Society thinks it's going right by you, that it's left you altogether. But if you're doing dynamic things mentally, the fact is that you can just put your foot out like that and the whole big ship of state is going to go. So, I said, "Call me Trim Tab."
>
> The truth is that you get the low pressure to do things, rather than getting on the other side and trying to push the bow of the ship around. And you build that low pressure by getting rid of a little

nonsense, getting rid of things that don't work and aren't true until you start to get that trim-tab motion. It works every time. That's the grand strategy you're going for. So, I'm positive that what you do with yourself, just the little things you do yourself, these are the things that count. To be a real trim tab, you've got to start with yourself, and soon you'll feel that low pressure, and suddenly things begin to work in a beautiful way. Of course, they happen only when you're dealing with really great integrity."

CHAPTER 31

BS Issue - Over Celebrating

"Wow, great job," quipped the out-of-touch executive who had no idea what he was recognizing someone for. He listed several accolades that this person didn't do. He continued and highlighted a few accomplishments that others on the team (who weren't recognized) did instead. Even though inaccurate, the cultural norm in this organization was to celebrate these "great" accomplishments for this person. Here, there was a clerical mistake, and the recognized person was supposed to be on the "not recognized" list. The recognized people were swapped with this list somewhere along the way.

Now, the intent here was to highlight and recognize those who went above and beyond. However, the opposite happened. This shift resulted in demoralizing an entire team, who soon left the company. As you may have guessed, the company never owned up to this, as the leaders who submitted the list didn't want to embarrass the executives. Apparently, that was more important than recognizing the team.

Now, let's be clear: this is a nuanced BS issue, and appropriate celebration is often missing in many workplaces. Genuine, honest, direct appreciation for the efforts and results people make can be lost in the cog of the machine. This section is not focused on healthy, productive, appropriate celebration events.

Instead, I suggest that over-celebrating might result in a lot more negative consequences for the corporate culture than may be apparent. When a celebration is cheapened, for example, it has less meaning to people. When we see the mediocre being celebrated as if it's the best thing ever, it's challenging for high performers to be a part of. To be dramatic for a moment, when something like showing up and the basics of your job has the same recognition for someone as another who discovered something new, created a solution, got it funded, taught a team, brought it to fruition and produced new results - it's a major demotivator.

Greg the Tyrant

"Wow, great job, Greg," said the executive in an early morning meeting. Once again, Greg recommended that the company do nothing and revisit things in six months. Greg had delivered dozens of these presentations, and they were almost all the same. His memo was filled with very poor grammar, lots of typos and no insights or data to back things up. To his credit, Greg had figured out that nothing was what the executives wanted to hear. That, or he got lucky. Greg was celebrated with verbal accolades and also got away with absolute brutality to coworkers and his direct leaders. He clearly thought he was too good for everyone else and was rewarded for it. "It's really great that we have great minds like this in our company," said another executive.

A few weeks later, it was someone else's turn to deliver an executive recommendation. After working many months at a solution, talking to peer companies, and consulting with vendors and industry experts, they had a solution to fix something plaguing the company for decades. It would require an investment, but that was relatively small. It would require some different thinking and approaches, which was perhaps the hardest for this organization to swallow. The presenter spent weeks with 1-1s and information sessions, so the executives and their teams had awareness this was coming. It was not a surprise. The presenter took more initiative than "just do nothing" and deeply cared about the organization's success. As he started off, Greg interrupted. Nobody stopped Greg. With no reasoning, data or points other than his opinion, he said, "Yeah, I don't think this will work." That was it, then silence. No executive jumped in to share a different perspective or suggest that they hear this presenter out. I sometimes imagine the presenter thinking of how they would respond to this, with a range of things that would work well in the next Terminator or Avenger movies.

Other than "do nothing," Greg had no solutions. In ten years, Greg had led no projects or efforts. He routinely belittled people and got away with doing it because nobody knew what to do with him. His "do nothing" mantra probably made some executives very comfortable, whether they were aware of this or not. Greg was celebrated and over-celebrated. New ideas that would help were not. Message received.

Celebration Balance

It's not always this blunt or brutal. Sometimes it's subtle. Maybe out of fear or not wanting to handle challenging situations, over-celebrating can occur. Leaders can begin to celebrate people just showing up as a major event as a big deal. Some of this is because some of the more in-demand roles are hard to find talent for. This can lead to prima donna syndrome which doesn't help anyone. While people should all be treated well and set up for a win (within reason), companies really shouldn't exist only to stroke the egos of the "smartest" people. Those same companies can be remiss in appreciating the simple but important things – like those who make sure the bathrooms are clean or arrange the catered lunches. They can also miss thanking those who are looking a few steps ahead of everyone else to make sure the company doesn't head into major troubling events.

Let's also be clear: there may be people we don't like who receive and deserve accolades. Just because we don't like them isn't a reason for the company not to reward them, although our brains can make that up. This would be a popularity contest, which can lead to the same over-celebrated (or wrongly celebrated) issues. We can also, as humans, become jealous and feel like we should be celebrated, but we aren't. Maybe we should and maybe we shouldn't - it's important to watch this energy.

When in doubt, think of one simple thing you are thankful for about someone else at work and tell them. This is direct, honest, in the moment and builds a positive culture. It also gets our minds off of how we were wronged or what we believe we deserve. When we realize these direct, often peer-to-peer accolades are more valuable than some constructed corporate contest, we are already winning. When you do this, you also set an example for someone else to do the same.

If you want it to land best, take a few extra moments to think about how the receiver will best receive the thanks. If they are introverted, something smaller and not so loud would probably be best. If they are extroverted, the big recognition and lots of people around would serve them. This is a slight tweak and doesn't take but a few moments to do. It has the added benefit of serving the people you want to celebrate and thank.

CHAPTER 32

Skill - Get Others to Problem Solve

Often, the workplace can seem filled with problem creation. There's a big new issue with a key client: legal is delayed on reviewing something, one of your key staff members is out sick, one of your vendors is not delivering again, and someone is whining in your daily standup. Sound familiar? That's how a lot of us start our workdays. Some start even earlier with a 2 am wakeup for a system outage.

In addition to these problems, there can be the problem of peers and leaders not knowing what to do when certain things are out of whack. They may turn to you as a known quantity to fix things. While this may be fun at times, having to solve everyone else's problems continually can be overwhelming and exhausting. It also means you get to deal with all of their shit. Not fun.

One way out of this is to get them to problem solve instead of you having to do this all the time. While some of you might drop an expletive when you read that, stay with me for a bit. There are some easy ways to get there and change what your workday looks like. What most high achievers do is start to filter out what they might consider noise. If a co-worker complains a lot with no solutions, we can maneuver around them. Sometimes, this goes for doing their work for them, so we don't have to endure that noise. This is like the early group work in high school, where the higher performers would often do the work for those not engaged on their team. While it would be wonderful if the entire team all decided to do well, we've all been on those classroom teams that seem to have some members who seem to care less if they get an F or an A, right?

Okay, let's dive into the brain structure briefly here. Earlier in the book, we talked about how all our senses route through the base of our brain. If the sensations aren't interrupted as fight/flight or freeze, they progress through our limbic system. If our limbic system isn't overloaded with these, the activity flows into our cerebral cortex. This is the area where problem-solving, creativity, collaboration and other high functions hang out. However, this might not be where the problem-creator often hangs out. Now, why you may not be motivated to help them given the upset in their delivery or attitudes, you can be motivated to help yourself out. Wouldn't it be nice if they solved more of their issues and maybe even some of yours?

But the brain-based techniques I used with success with my autistic son, and which I wrote about in *Unleashed*, work for all humans. When we can get someone to a calm state, then have them recognize our concern, and then ask them to problem solve, we will be astounded by the results. It's highly repeatable, science-backed and evidence-based.

There are three steps to this, and it's based on the decades of work by Dr. Ross Greene (63):

1. Empathy and Validation
2. State Your Concern
3. Ask Them To Problem Solve (and Take Action)

Okay, in our tired and frustrated state, we can jump to try to force problem-solving and quick action. We can be surprised that others aren't ready to do this yet. They must be lazy slackers. Why don't they get it?

The science behind this shows that people want to do well. I know that's hard to believe. I struggle with that daily - "Really, him? He wants to do well?" The data in the studies is clear. Certain situations get people stuck in their primitive brain or limbic brain - and they literally cannot fully access their problem-solving functions. Have you ever been so upset you literally couldn't see straight? In that state, are you able to problem-solve or handle complex things? Of course not. The same is true for others - and they may not be showing you the clues for you to know that they aren't in the best state of mind.

The good news here is that you can help others build up their skills, and it's relatively easy. Now, it takes some effort and engaging with people you may not prefer. That part stops a lot of us, and trust me, I get it.

However, when we do this - and it's a few minutes at a time - the results are consistent. When I first heard about all of this, even with the brain science and studies, I was super skeptical. Begrudgingly, I tried this with my son, who struggled. Now, I know that goes to a parent-child relationship. However, I can tell you the same process works with your co-workers. Yes, even them.

...

On another gloomy day, after a hectic commute, I edged up to pick up my son. I also cringed, knowing that I'd likely hear some story about him acting out. This school was poorly equipped to serve his special needs. Even worse, he was triggered by many of their approaches.

Almost in shock, there was no report from the teacher who helped him in the car. She must have forgotten or just had pity on me, I thought.

"Hey, Dad, can I tell you something?"

"Sure, what's up, buddy?"

"Hey, I'd like to tell you a big story and then tell you about my day. Is that okay?"

With tears welling up in my eyes, I told my little dude, "Yes, son."

The Blend Ends

For years, my son did what most with autism do - blend reality with fantasy. In his mind, he would literally see the Avengers in the classroom and maybe even interact with his imaginary friends. When you asked him how his day went, the story was mixed with what likely happened in school and a vibrant imagination. For a parent trying to understand what happened during the day, this was maddening. I could easily conclude that he was lying (which he wasn't doing).

For weeks, after learning a different approach that is brain-based, I made the extra effort to be more empathetic and validate him - even if I didn't agree. But over time, this helps kiddos like him to regulate and not be stuck in fight/flight/freeze. He's less of a prisoner of those primitive brain functions.

After many "microdoses" of empathy (as my instructor expertly explained the approach), I would express one simple adult concern like "safety". After hearing him out, he would seem to understand this much better. Then, finally, I would ask him to problem-solve.

The solutions were amazing and not things I would have ever thought of. Later, he started popping out solutions like he did on that rainy car pickup day.

To be clear - we had done dozens of approaches with him with very limited results. We did occupational therapy, traditional therapy, medications, probiotics, organic food, tough love, and things I don't even remember now. However, this brain-based approach made all the difference. Later, I tweaked it and used it with co-workers and my team. It created a culture that's hard to describe, other than problem-solving, is greatly increased, along with team output. When BS enters the system, it doesn't get stuck for long and is processed with several solutions. Even better, I don't have to create them or be the constant problem solver.

While this probably sounds like an infomercial, it isn't. And if you are skeptical, it's okay. I'm still in shock this works so well when I use it. So, here's the three steps to use. If you want to go deeper into this, there are a few recommended books and sites at the back of this book:

1. <u>Empathize and Validate.</u> You'll stay here for a few days, just a few minutes at a time. Do not pass go. Do not collect $200. It's tempting to rush through this. That generally gives crap results. You already have those, so stay with the fidelity here to get something else. When you ask something like, "Hey, that meeting seemed hard, what's going on?" just listen. You don't have to agree or even like what they say. It might piss you off. That's okay; just understand how true it is **for them**. You should not talk a lot here, but if you do, it's things like, "It makes sense you feel that way". You are not feeling sorry

for them; you are just listening and acknowledging. You also don't need to take on all their shit. Just empathize.

2. <u>State Your Concern.</u> After doing step 1 a few times (at least 3), you may be ready to progress to this state. Step one is already accomplishing a lot. You can stay there for a few weeks and still see the results. But, if you get to the place where your colleague feels heard and understood, ask, "Hey, is it okay if I share a concern?" Only if they say yes, will you share a concern. Now, here's the hard part - get your concern to one or two words. No, this isn't the time to share your sob story, but use a word like "safety" or "productivity" or something like this. Then, ask them if it makes sense to them. If it doesn't - go back to a few more step ones. Please remember concern is singular. Pick <u>one</u>.

3. <u>Problem Solving.</u> After completing steps one and two, you'll get here. It won't happen all the time. But, when it does, you'll start with something like, "Well, it sounds like I understand you, and you understand me - what ideas do you have to resolve this?"

After this, you go quiet. It might be uncomfortable. They might say nothing. They are building new muscles here. Resist your own solutioning. When they come up with their own solutions, they will eventually do a quick test. That test is simply to decide if that solution is workable for all parties - and what action steps you can take (right then or the next day).

These three steps are incredibly easy. The discomfort will happen for a bit, sure, but doesn't last for long. The results are contagious, and you may find your colleague unknowingly using this approach later with you and others. If you give people a chance to use their prefrontal cortex, the solutions they bring to bear are considerable. However, getting there can be a rough journey, and you may have to help them carve out a path. Yes, you may also have to let go of some beliefs about that person, too. It's okay, you can get them back if you need them - you aren't missing out.

CHAPTER 33

BS Issue - Excuses

"Letting things slide to keep the peace only starts a war inside of you."

— *Mel Robbins*

"We can't do that this year because we weren't funded for it."

Ever hear that excuse in response for not doing something critical for your workplace? Maybe it's something that has proven to bring more revenue in. Or this can be something to make customers happier or keep top employees around longer. Maybe it's something that your company loves to problem admire, almost like addicts. Whatever it is, if it's eating at you as an excuse, this is the BS thing for you. This can also be a power play in some organizations. Some leadership echelons will choose not to fund something just because they don't prefer it. It could have no attachment to the health of the company; it's just that they don't like it or understand it. Even in the modern workplace with sophisticated analytics and insights and modern leadership practices, big decisions may be structured to rely on executives only. Sometimes, these people are considerably out of touch with some details of their company. While well-intentioned, they may not know best. And, if they don't trust those who might know best in their organization, they may have committed themselves to a more rapid path to obsolescence.

Often, there are creative ways to make progress on goals in these situations. Yes, it will require diverse ideas and maybe some skunkworks. The organization may already have what it needs to make progress and needs to think and act slightly differently to accelerate this. Often, prototypes and working examples lead to some funding to help new ideas along as the momentum forms around it. It doesn't have to stagnate.

Get Scrappy or Accept Crappy

As a large, traditional, top-down employer, we faced some major challenges for our customer service organization. These are not unique, when we look at our peers. However, we knew we had to do something about it instead of being like everyone else. The customer service agents had to use and learn as many as two dozen applications on any phone call. Let that sink in. For the millions of annual calls this company received, over twenty-four applications were used on each call. This meant that onboarding new agents would take over six months until they were productive. They had to learn 24 applications and often copy/paste data between them to do their jobs. When they were human and made a mistake in this complex environment, it would result in wrong information being shared with a customer. Because of the industry, this could also lead to massive fines. One of the common measures used in these large call environments is handling time. This is generally how long the call was. Here, the average handle time was considerably longer than the norm. Much of this was believed to be due to the applications and the wrap-up time needed after the call. While the leadership of these teams did an amazing job of keeping morale up, the tooling to serve customers was second-rate.

Year after year, they created proposals to have this modernized. The business case was solid. However, the excuses for not funding this critical measure were consistent. At one point, the company did a large RFP for solutions in this space. Other teams in the organization gold-plated them so much that the quotes came to a staggering $12M for the first year. This greatly exceeded other projects in the portfolio and was considered too expensive. Meanwhile, the voice of the company continued to be that of customer service agents with very poor tools to do their jobs.

Instead of putting up with this BS, a few began to think out of the box. They looked at how they could use the tools that they already had to improve things. It might not be the entire $12M wish list, but there might also be things this team could at least experiment with and prototype in the meantime. In watching what the agents did, they realized that an existing analytics tool the company owned could probably help. While it wasn't normal to use this tool in this way, the use case lined right up. After a quick prototype and some fine-tuning, they tried it with a small percentage of the customer service team. While they got feedback to make a few tweaks, this first little prototype helped a great deal. Instead of nearly eight screens to go through to get everything to serve a customer, it was available on one screen and in a few seconds.

The team then discovered a few creative ways to add on some more of the wish list to this tool with a few simple web tools. It wasn't perfect and didn't serve all our needs, but it made the agent and customer experience much better. Those approaches cost only a little ingenuity and some staff time. This initial work saved 10-15% of the average handle time. The company had to invest in more license seats for this analytics tool, but they could use their divisional budget for it. The prototype created savings they could use. Instead of $12M, it was $300k. That spending was easy to get approved because they had a working solution and a pathway to introduce more.

Now, I'll be the first to tell you that this solution wasn't pretty, but it was functional. It didn't have the technical elegance that my architecture friends would prefer, but it also worked amazingly well. And, even with its many faults and shortcomings, it won a major industry reward, besting major organizations like Comcast and major retailers.

Because of the success of this effort, the team later found a way to get a few more staff members and a more appropriate Customer Relationship Management (CRM) solution. They prototyped this on a small scale. They did not rely on the central funding function that had denied their requests for many years. While this did require more funding to implement, it turned out to be less than 10% of the $12M that was thought to be needed. The handful of people who worked on this received the company's top honors in a highly coveted peer-to-peer award.

Iterations Win

The big story here is really a little thing - instead of accepting the circumstance of no funding - they knew they had a need and found a way to take small actions. Instead of going with problem admiration (and accepting that status quo of their needs being too expensive), they prototyped and came up with a model 10% of the expected costs.

As daunting as big company problems can be, along with the myths, folklore, and BS-inflated budgets they purportedly have, there's almost always another way to make progress. And often, it may be faster, better and less expensive. And yes, I know that defies a project management mantra of pick one - faster, better or cheaper. When the excuses are let go of, and immediate action is prioritized, creative and innovative approaches can bust that top-down triangle intended to create limits. As the work progresses, this triangle can be a tool for fine tuning. But, as an upfront measure, before work starts, it can stall many exceptional programs.

Chapter Exercise

1. List 3-5 important efforts that your company refuses to fund or act on. It's even better if these ideas get you fired up, and if you know there's a way to make progress on them somehow.

2. List all the reasons that you believe action isn't being taken today. Funding, staffing and resources are common. Also look for the rare ones. Are their belief systems or favorites that seem to get funded over others?

3. Think of who would benefit from even small actions taken. Is it employees, customers, business partners? What benefits would they have? Are there any revenue-creating or cost-saving ones? If there are, do a quick estimate of what you think they are. Pro tip - don't share this number because we often overestimate things. I would recommend 25-30% of that number to be used. This also makes breakout results easier to demonstrate.

4. Think of who can help you make a working prototype here. Now, working prototypes can be as simple as drawings and

storyboards. They can also be basic applications with very limited features.

5. Get them excited, find time (yes, it might be after hours) and see what you can do in a couple of weeks (or less). If it's good, identify a few leaders to show it to, along with your analysis.

6. In your presentation, lead with the demo. Way too many people give a long PowerPoint. Leaders are drowning in PowerPoint. Start with the demo.

7. If you encounter a very busy leader's schedule, make a short video of your demo. It doesn't have to be fancy. Free tools like Loom make this easy. Sending a link to a short video with a thumbnail image is more likely to be seen than a PowerPoint, word attachment, or long email.

8. Know that you may have to rinse/repeat here to show different demos. You are the trim tab here, helping your giant tanker of a company to maneuver. You'll move fast and they take longer.

9. Even if no actions are taken, you have demonstrated yourself to be an innovator. When reviews and opportunities come up, you'll be on a short list selected for those efforts. If nothing else, you positioned yourself for a raise. You also have a great story for your next employer and maybe even a book someday.

CHAPTER 34

Skill - Follow the Customer

On a busy day, confused by a slew of new priorities coming to our team, I vented with my boss in our 1-1. My brain was mush, and it seemed like new work was coming at us from every direction. All were apparently urgent new needs. What he said didn't make sense at least in the context he meant it, but it does now. What did he say?

"Follow the money, Chris."

In my stressed-out state, I wasn't cognizant enough to get his wisdom. If I were, I would have known he suggested that I prioritize things that most align with the company generating revenue... and maybe how they spend it too. Much of the time, it's easy to get caught up in what our boss or employer *isn't* doing for us, and we can forget the money flow at our companies. We can also forget our customers, who are the ones truly paying us.

> *"It's not the employer who pays the wages. Employers only handle the money. It's the customer who pays the wages."*
>
> *-Henry Ford*

Because of this, I'd like to suggest expanding on this "follow the money" guidance a bit further to "follow the customer". One way to measure this is called customer lifetime value (CLV). This measure looks at all the spending a customer may have with a company over their lifetime, and not just a single transaction. In this model, organizations look to see how they can develop multiple purchases and relationships with their customers that last. Entire strategies can even involve losing money on the first transactions with a customer to gain a long-term customer. You can see this in the retail space, where a low-priced item or special deal gets the customer in the door (or on their website) to buy. While there, they may buy more or join a subscription after a great first experience.

In a more glaring way, you can see this approach on social media ads with what are called funnels. There's some compelling, inexpensive book or webinar that gets our attention for a small price like $7. It gets us to stop scrolling on our social media and to buy. The ad writers here are skilled at targeting people with specific needs and riling up emotions quickly. As part of the online sales process, they will offer you some "one-time" deals. These are normally additional products like classes or more of the same product at a discounted price (think 3 bags of dog food for 50% off if you buy now). The copy will read something like, "If you really want to get the best out of this, you'll get this too." In this buying emotional state, while it may be a small percentage, enough people buy these add-ons. Those who don't buy them will receive several emails that entice them also to buy more. Entire companies focus on this process and science. The process creates billions more for companies than just a focus on selling a single product. In fact, often that up-front starter product costs the same amount as the customer acquisition costs (i.e., ad spend). While the company may lose money on the first purchases here, the upsells and long-term customer relationship, or CLV, is what they are after.

Now, I'm not suggesting you need to become a master marketer or marketing funnel creator, but you can use curiosity to help you out here when it feels like you are drowning in urgent tasks.

Here are five steps you can take to focus and follow the customer at your organization:

1. **Draw out a simple diagram.** Start with a new customer. How do they hear about your company? How do they buy things from you? If you don't know, find people you can ask about this.

2. On the diagram, **draw a simple picture of how this customer is onboarded** and provisioned. Does this go through a number of systems? Do they pay with a credit card? How does their information go into other systems? Are people involved? You might be surprised at the number of spreadsheets and emails that might go along with what you may think should be automated.

3. If you can, on this same diagram, **map out how an additional sale to this customer may occur.** Is it an email reach out? Do ads get them excited to buy? Are there different products for them? For example, if you are a car dealership, you may find that the service department has an entire strategy after a vehicle is sold.

4. Now, it's time to **add the flow for when the customer may need to return something.** How do they do this? Is it phone, web, automated or in-person? What are your policies here? Do you restock the item or ship it to be auctioned? How often does this occur?

5. After you have this diagram, **highlight where you already affected the process today**. Even if it's indirect, note this. Also note where you think you could help more or have ideas to help.

Now that you have this diagram, it's time to reflect. Instead of focusing on the BS of the day or how poorly you may be treated, you have a different focus for a bit. This activity does not validate the BS-ery that you are experiencing. We are putting that aside for a moment. As part of this exercise, you will have talked to a few different people in the organization. What's amazing is how rarely people ask these questions and draw these pictures out. Your diagram and new knowledge has become a big company asset.

There are two sets of actions you can do with this drawing:

1. **Prioritize your current work.** Look at the diagram to see what you have already done. Where can you do things differently to best affect the customer? With your diagram, suggest to your co-workers and boss ideas you must make this happen. They may be small at first. However, instead of an artificial deliverable like a status report or meeting, you are tracking against items that improve the world for your customer. Even if your current employer doesn't get it, many others will welcome this simple approach. One word of caution here - this work will expose areas that aren't as customer-focused or beneficial. Some hide in these organizations for decades and are defensive. You don't need to shine a bright light in their caves and arouse angry bears, just do your own thing.

2. **Think of new work.** On your diagram, and as you do this work, there may be other things that excite you. It may not align with your existing work. There may be part of the organization doing some things here... or maybe nobody is even thinking about it. Because this excites you and helps the customer, this is a great place to plan your career trajectory. While you can go with whatever projection there is in your department and move from level I to level II to level III - you could also explore where this work may take you. Because it's of higher value to the organization, these usually come with higher pay increases and a higher likelihood you are working on what you love. This part will require that you create a few talking points, do some research so you have insights and analytics to back your excitement, and in the best case - even a prototype. A prototype can be a drawing on paper, or it can be a simple working model if you are so inclined. It may take you showing this idea a few times for excitement to get going. Some might not get it. And, if your company doesn't want to engage, know others do. Your specific knowledge here is valuable. The skill of following the customer is, too.

The skill of following the customer can greatly help our mindset as well. Instead of focusing on the dread at work, we are in solution-creation mode. We can't always hop to another job right away, given the circumstances of our lives. This doesn't mean we have to stay stuck though. In addition, the mindset shift, you may find you created a whole new role at your company that may not entirely suck. It may have a different set of leadership you can more easily work with. And, even if your current employer doesn't choose to act on your great ideas, you have built a skillset and a great story for your next employer.

Imagine saying something like "I put together a program to increase customer purchases by 15% and increase their satisfaction by 25%, and I'd love to collaborate with a company that wants to take advantage of these gains." That's a lot more compelling than a list of skills and having a mediocre answer for, "Why are you leaving."

Follow the customer.

CHAPTER 35

BS Issue - Ethical Issues

Before we dive in here, let's be super clear. A range of ethical issues can come up in the workplace. Most organizations have a code of conduct to explain what matters to them. There are also Federal, State and local laws that may be at play in your situation. Some of these work ethical issues are obvious, egregious and blatant. Those obvious issues are more straightforward to deal with. In my experience, though, most of the ethical issues in the workplace are more subtle. The code of conduct might not be clear on these issues, and the evidence might be mediocre. The laws may also not be clear. There is usually a lot of gray. However, these are still issues.

While a recent study found that ethics are improving in the workplace, the score doesn't sound great. According to this report, "1 in 5 US employees were in workplaces with a strong ethical culture, compared with 1 in 10 in 2000. Globally, 14% of employees are working in organizations with a strong ethical culture." (64) While 10% is better than 5%, this still means that 90% of those surveyed think their companies do not have a strong ethical culture. If we were grading this, that's an A for *bad* culture in the workplace. Often, this occurs, and we're not sure what to really do about it. While it may feel like snitching, we still have an urge that something isn't right, and it eats at us.

Collusion

At a previous employer, a director on a different team apparently had a large side business. This isn't an issue if it doesn't interfere with the company, right? Well, his side hustle was a staff augmentation firm. This means they provided contractors and temporary talent to companies who needed it. Generally, these contractors are billed out at 2x to 3x what they are paid. So, if they make $50/hour, their company charges $150/hour. Yes, it can be a lucrative business. After I had left this company, I learned this director sourced contractors for projects only he knew about. These weren't yet shared publicly to the normal hiring channels. He had inside information on these roles, and his side hustle company won most of the contracting business due to this. Even worse, he used his role to advocate for projects that his side company could handle. How that happened in this highly regulated company, or how that director thought this was okay, frankly stuns me. It's one of dozens of examples we can probably all think of.

What Ethics Do People Care About?

According to a study at Florida Tech (65) and a global business ethics survey (66), are five types of issues that matter most to employees regarding ethics:

1. **Unethical Accounting** - The big stories here are situations where major accounting firms worked with large companies, like Enron, and knowingly recorded fake entries to benefit them. Enron closed, resulting in over 85,000 people out of work and $25B in losses for investors. While these situations may seem like outliers, major financial firms have billions in fines for their unethical schemes (67). To name a few:

a) JP Morgan Chase Ponzi Scheme with Bernie Madoff - $1.7B restitution

b) Credit Suisse Tax Fraud - $2.5B in fines

c) Wells Fargo Phantom Accounts - $3B in fines

d) Wells Fargo Overcharging Customers - $3.7B in fines

e) Goldman Sachs money laundering $5.4B

f) JP Morgan Chase and Bank of America Subprime scandals - $34.6B combined.

2. **Social Media Ethics** - With more and more of us working remotely, and on our devices, what is acceptable to post about work and what isn't? While we do have free speech and freedom of expression, does a personal post count as libel now? Or, differently, is what someone does in their non-work time, if it's on social media, in the purview of the company? This gets complex quickly, and defining what's reasonable and the right thing is gray at best.

3. **Harassment and Discrimination** - While we'd like to think we have evolved past this, harassment and discrimination continue in the workplace. According to the US Equal Opportunity Employment Commission (EEOC) over $505M in fines were collected in 2019 for victims of discrimination (68). Similarly, a recent study by the University of California Hasting School of Law found that cases of harassment and discrimination have increased 269% over the last decade. (69) These figures only reflect the situations where this behavior was actually reported or tried.

4. **Health and Safety** - While there are lots of regulations and policies to help with workplace injuries, there are still many fatalities. In the UK, nearly 7400 people die a year from work-related issues (70). In the US, according to the US Bureau of Labor Statistics, there were nearly 5500 workplace deaths in 2022, and over 2.8M workplace injuries in that same year. (71)

5. **Technology and Privacy** - While companies can (and do) monitor workplace computer and internet use, many are not aware this is the case. This can get complex when using a personal device - cell phone, laptop, tablet - to remotely access your company. The question of who owns this data and who owns your time is a more complex topic in a remote workforce.

So, with all these issues and figures, what should you do? It's simple. If you think an issue at your workplace violates your or your company's ethics, report it. Now, this is not a time to be vindictive and "get" someone. If you legitimately feel there is an ethics issue, find out how to anonymously report it. And, if you are a victim of one of these ethical issues, document everything. You may need to lawyer up to be aware of your options. And, while the movies have great stories of the little guy sticking it to the man even if we are in the "right," the timeline to get any meaningful results can be long and expensive. Be aware of what you are in for. Depending on your situation, you may need to decide if your fight is worth it, or your energy is better spent elsewhere.

CHAPTER 36

Skill - Draw a Picture and Use Insights

Here it comes again. Another long email string back and forth. After many meetings and discussions, it seems like they just don't get it. They don't seem to understand what we are doing and why. Aren't they supposed to support us? WTF!?

Onboarding a new technology and approach, I had a gauntlet of approvals to go through. Some of these people in these phase gates had no incentive to approve anything. Thinking differently was not one of their specialties. So, explaining innovation was especially fun when they didn't understand yet that "the old way" was majorly broken.

My team had a new approach with a somewhat subtle change that would benefit external customers and reduce internal costs. This approach was relatively easy but apparently required more of a mindset shift than we expected. Finally, it clicked what the problem was - we were being verbal (and written) with our request.

Drawing The Picture

"Mitch, can you draw a picture of this?" I asked my frustrated colleague.

"Yeah, but I don't think they'll look at it." he quipped back.

"You might be right, but what do we have to lose?" I answered.

"Good point," said Mitch.

Mitch worked on a simple diagram. We improved it a little together, adding more detail. I made talking points to share. At our next review sessions with the approval bodies, I shared the drawing. I started with something like, "Hey, we know this might not make sense at first, so we drew this picture to explain it better."

After a few short bits of discussion, clearly a lightbulb went off for that review team. While it was obvious to my team, until the reviewers saw this picture, they just didn't get it.

"Oh, that makes sense now. Why didn't you do that before?" asked the reviewers.

I was just quiet as they said "approved" soon after this question.

What was literally months, dozens of meetings, and probably hundreds of emails were solved by this simple drawing.

5 Easy Steps (Even if You are not an Artist)

You don't need to be an artist to do this, and you can always get help, too. Wherever possible, I encourage everyone to make a drawing about what you are asking for. One reason for this is that everyone has different learning modalities. Some people cannot take in information as easily when it's verbal or written. Others may just zone out, and a picture engages a different part of their brain.

Here are easy steps to take to do this at your work:

1. Make a simple sketch first on your own. This can be on scrap paper, or in PowerPoint, or in a free online drawing program like Miro.
2. On this simple sketch, just use boxes, arrows and maybe stick figures for people.

3. After you draw it, notice if anything else should be included or if the diagram should be reworked. You aren't going for perfection here. If the boxes don't perfectly line up, it's okay right now.

4. Have a colleague you trust take a quick look and listen to their input. Even if you don't agree with them, realize that others might take the information the way they did. Make updates if you can.

5. Create talking points and ask for 5 minutes to present this at the next meeting (or schedule the meeting). Lead with the drawing and maybe share it in advance. Notice the engagement you get and actions being different.

Lights, Camera Action

Now, if you have an especially busy work environment, or an executive whose calendar is booked out for weeks (or months), there's another tool you can use - short videos. While this might give you some anxiety about being on camera or worrying about saying the wrong thing, it's a lot easier than you may imagine. You can use a feature in Microsoft Teams or a free tool like Loom to do this.

In your video, you will be crisp and simple - think 60 seconds. Your script will say something like, "Hey, Bubba, it's Chris. I know you are swamped, and I wanted to bounce this off of you because I think you'd want to know about it. My request is that we fund this effort at $10k, and the benefits are 25% faster response times and a projected 15% increase in customer satisfaction. Let me walk you through this picture real fast."

You'll be surprised at what a great response you'll get from these. Instead of emails and voicemails never returned, you'll get a quick message back from them, usually with approval or a few steps they would like to see. You won't have to wait weeks or months for a meeting. When you do this, you are also honoring how busy your executives may be. You are also saving them (and yourself) from another long meeting. They'll also appreciate your innovation. Now, if you are talking about something secret to your company, use tools (like MS Teams) that are approved and internal only - something like Loom might violate your privacy rules.

If you need to, you can also stack these videos and trickle feed your executive. For example, send one on Monday, then Tuesday, then Wednesday. This can be a great way to prepare an executive before a meeting and give you more face time. It also lets them watch these short videos while they are on the go – no matter what time zone they are in or where they are traveling to.

So, when in doubt… actually, all the time - make a quick picture to describe what you want to do or are doing. You'll get quicker approvals and agreements and be able to move forward faster. And, if you want even better results, try short videos to communicate.

Get Insightful

Now that you have some basic visuals and perhaps a short video to help encourage movement on issues and projects, let's talk insights. Before we dive into this, I want to mention a nuance, or maybe it's a pet peeve - the word data. You'll hear "use data" often from those talking about using insights. To get clear on definitions here, data is a giant transaction log or spreadsheet with thousands of rows. Data is a flow of information that is recorded but rarely has any meaning. The analysis of that data, or insights derived from it, are what we use and want. Data is important, to be sure. However, a big list of all of Amazon's transactions will not mean as much as a chart that shows which products sold where and when, along with trends. Once more, as much as we think we are rational decision-makers, we now know that our emotion-driven limbic system is a massive part of all decisions. So, how we share the insights and the story about them can help equip your audience to act.

Insights come in many shapes, and it's interesting how some don't question them. I'm not advocating lying to people and coming up with fake insight points to prove a BS story here. Please don't do that. We already have enough. However, I suggest that, assuming you have good intentions, find data points that may help support your perspective. As you do this work, you may need to refine your points based on the insights you are now learning from. Here are four places you can find sources:

1. Search Engines - This is the go-to for most people. They'll Google something, look on the first page for a source. They will probably find a quote they like and stop there. This isn't necessarily a bad thing and can be a good place to start. Realize, though, that there's an entire engine trying to please you with what you want. It may not be sharing the blind spots of things wrong with your perspective. Knowing those can help refine your solution to be stronger.

2. Guidance Experts - Companies like Gartner and Forrester publish thousands of articles on technology and business topics. I used to joke you could find a quote for anything on Gartner. Jokes aside, if you are in the tech space especially,

they have a "magic quadrant" that has become almost a de facto tool in software selections. While there are paid versions of their services, you can find many articles that are complementary.

3. <u>Specialized News Sources</u> - Publications like the Harvard Business Review carry a lot of credibility and can be great sources for many insights on the people and financial side of changes. You will find groups on LinkedIn in your niche that may also serve you here.

4. <u>Peers </u>- This can be a tricky one. Your peers may be in a competitive space and cannot share company secrets. However, either within your company (like a different division), or a colleague at another company (who can share information) can be a great ally and information source. A few sound bites from them - and that you consulted a peer - strengthens any proposal. Another option here is to ask your vendor, or prospective vendor, to connect you with a reference customer. They may have several they can connect you with.

Now, when you think of insights, you may be thinking dashboards and charts, right? Yep, me too. So why the text and story-based stuff first? Even with the best data visualizations, you'll need a story to bring it home. We love stories and storytellers. Having someone walk us through the visualization, with a story and a few key points, makes a much larger impact than sending a link to a chart and hoping for the best.

Now, on data visualizations, at least at first, you can focus on trends and outliers. This means the data behind it may not be perfect. Yes, you may be blessed with perfect data for your work, and if so, congrats! However, most of us have data that is good enough to find trends and outliers, but not for audited financial reports to give the SEC. At least, not at first.

I share this so you don't get stuck. While you don't want to rely on averages of averages too much, knowing the shape and directions of the data is more important. This means to focus on whether things are going up or down and what sorts of things are outside the norm. If you can, consider what you believe influences these changes and the outliers. While I do recommend you use more precise data to measure your progress on efforts going forward, for your initial take, you are focused on direction, speed, and outliers.

Geeking out for a second, this approach uses a physics principle - the Heisenberg Uncertainty Principle. This principle states "Formulated by the German physicist and Nobel laureate Werner Heisenberg in 1927, the uncertainty principle states that we cannot know both the position and speed of a particle, such as a photon or electron, with perfect accuracy; the more we nail down the particle's position, the less we know about its speed and vice versa." (72)

Okay, if I lost you here (sorry), simply put, this means you can know the exact position or direction of something, but not both. If we equate this to insights early on in an effort, we'll have the direction but not the exact position. As we do the work and get more precise data, we'll be able to determine the position (but not the direction). If we focus on perfect data and analytics first - we won't have the trend and can get stuck. It's okay to have slightly lower fidelity at first with your insights - and it may even help your effort move. Also, if a data expert questions your initial insights, you can let them know you are using quantum physics and the Heisenberg

Uncertainty Principle. Then, ask for their help for the data approach they recommend, refining your insights and findings.

CHAPTER 37

BS Issue - Pretending It's Okay

> *"If a lie is only printed often enough, it becomes a quasi-truth, and if such a truth is repeated often enough, it becomes an article of belief, a dogma, and men will die for it."*
>
> *— Isa Blagden*

This quote is often attributed to Lenin (and others). However, it is sourced from a book Blagden published in 1869. The quote is probably attributed to others because of their propaganda campaigns that built their rise to power.

Luckily, most of our workplaces don't resemble this sort of extreme. However, even in less combative environments, the pattern is the same. In modern studies, they even found that even those with earlier knowledge and experience can be affected by this "illusion of truth" (68). In a somewhat stunning bit of research, experts from Vanderbilt, Duke and UNC Chapel Hill found "Contrary to prior suppositions, illusory truth effects occurred even when participants knew better." So even though we might know and be experts in something, this effect can result in believing in a group norm instead. Their studies showed that participants demonstrated "the failure to rely on stored knowledge in the face of fluent processing experiences."

Death By PowerPoint

Blue, fluorescent lights buzzed and flickered in the large meeting room. The silence was awkward and strangely deafening. We would look up, maybe make eye contact, then look down. Nobody wanted to be here. Every seat was taken, and people had pulled a mish-mash of chairs in, so they had a place to sit. We all seemed to be eying the doors as an emergency escape should we need to bolt. A few minutes later, a couple of executives sauntered into the room. As they dribbled out some sort of hello, the crowd attempted a mumble that closely resembled "hello". Some may have been stopping their gag reflex.

"Today we're going over the results that show how things came out in our recent employee survey," quipped one of the suits.

Glances passed between team members. We knew it was rigged. A few butt-kissers had planned comments to share to make their leaders and themselves look good. I snickered under my breath and remembered a previous game of buzzword bingo. This is where you put bingo cards with most often use corp-speak phrases on them. If you ever do this, pro tip, refrain from shouting "bingo" during a meeting. Big thanks to Frank Ledo for keeping this alive and creating free online tools to create these cards (74). This is probably what that card would have looked like on that day.

Integration	Forward-Thinking	Bottom-Line	Positive	At The End Of The Day
Culture	Survey	Industry	Engagement	Leadership
Opportunity	Ownership	COLLABORATION (free square)	Results	Leading
Satisfaction	Innovative	Supportive	Peers	Insights
Inclusive	Average	Collaborate	Double-Click	Double-Down

The executive showed us charts showing how great they thought the culture was. We couldn't see some of it because the projector in that room had long lost the ability to project red. Blue and yellow came through nicely though. Along with the projector issues, we noticed that the hard questions were missing from this presentation. Somehow those measures didn't seem to make it to the slide deck.

Another presenter joined in. They were from a consulting firm. They showed charts on how our company was better than our peers. Based on our experience, this seemed suspect. Even the old fluorescent lights seemed to flicker with disgust.

Thankfully, the meeting ended, and we got back to our cubes.

A little later that day, the company announced that it had been selected as a top place to work. Their social media was full of these announcements. These announcements had several photos, but none were of actual company employees. They had chosen stock photos that more resembled the message they were trying to sell others.

While this sounds like madness, and perhaps was, I'm sure many of you have been at organizations where the leaders are out of touch. Maybe the workplace even believes the story they are telling - either out of illusion of truth, or fear of retaliation, or exhaustion - the workplace becomes an echo chamber.

At this same workplace, we later did one of those assessments that assigns you a color and a letter (and even an animal). It found that 90%+ of the workers valued indirect communication only and had a great resistance to change. The other 10% in the room all looked at each other and nodded quietly - we still somehow thought we could make things better in this culture. However, we likely had a much better chance at buzzword bingo.

Staying at a place like this for too long can be dangerous to your sanity. We all have times in our lives where we may feel we need to be in survival mode. However, do your best to contain this with some milestone dates (i.e., on August 1st, I will look at opportunities again). Also, network with others outside of your workplace. You may also want to find a nonprofit you can donate time to, to give your energy a positive place to be.

And, if you catch yourself caught up in sharing corporate mistruths, get yourself back on track. Your integrity is more important than your paycheck. It may take some effort and a little time, but you need not stay stuck in the cell with the flickering lights.

CHAPTER 38

Skill - Networking In the Clicky Clicky Age

When I want to find something, what's my go-to? For me, it's become Google or Alexa.

When I was looking to book a hotel on a business trip, I expected Google to direct me to the right place. This was a remote area and a small hotel that didn't show up on the normal travel sites.

When I found that the place didn't offer a way to book online, I got upset. But I had to use this phone feature on my phone to make what is called a call. How archaic!

Sound familiar?

This pattern carries over into how many of us have morphed to interact.

In applying to jobs, we can apply to dozens (maybe hundreds) of jobs in LinkedIn and be surprised nobody replies to us. Behind the scenes, a lot of those jobs aren't available. Many companies have policies they must post a job externally, just so they can promote someone. So, the likelihood of an external candidate disrupting this, even if they are the most stellar on the planet, is low. Some HR systems (all digital) aren't looking for the right keywords or they aren't in the right place on the resume to be found. And sometimes, a company wants to convert a contractor to a full-time employee, and they must post a job. While it's listed somewhere, it isn't an available position.

However, when there is a job available, does an online application get attention just by clicking submit? Not really.

Here are staggering statistics for those who are confused as to why clicking only on job searches isn't producing results:

- 85% of jobs are filled through networking. (75)
- 70% of jobs are never published publicly. (76)
- 70% of professionals hired had a connection at their company (77)

Okay, so at least regarding job hunting, networking and relationships matter, maybe more than massive applying activities (clicky clicky). In our work from anywhere in the world now, how do you do that? We're on Zoom, Google or MS Teams sessions, and many don't even turn on their camera, so we're talking to a black screen.

For people like me, who are introverts and work extra to be super social, networking can feel like a chore. If that's you, just remember you are going for a result here, and it might not be as bad as you think. For those of you who are super social and love this, you may already have networking down and are thinking, "What's the big deal?"

Here's a few tips and ideas to help boost your networking skills - both at your current job and outside of it:

At Your Current Job:

- Make one list. List people in your company that you don't yet know well or want to know better.
- Create an action plan. Once a week, contact a few people on your list. This can be a call, email, or your company's internal chat.
- Your reach-out should be something light like "Hey, I would love to hear how project X is going and what's new in the Y division. Do you have 15 minutes to talk on X? Okay for me to grab time on your calendar?"
- When on the call, listen. Let them talk most of the time. Have questions ready to understand things more. If you have ideas of ways you could help, quickly note them and bring them up at the end of the call.
- Within 24 hours, follow-up with them. Thank them for the time, and have your action items done or at least started.
- Finally, if you don't already, seek a mentor at your company. This can be an executive or really anyone. It's ideal if they are outside of your current reporting tree. So, if you can find a manager, director, VP or C-level that you don't report up through, that's ideal. Find someone you feel is strong in a space that maybe you aren't yet. Contact them and ask for help. Leaders love to feel like they are creating solutions and helping. Play to that.

Outside Your Current Job:

- Make two lists. List people you already know and want to strengthen your relationship with. Then list people you don't yet know but want to meet (and later strengthen your relationship with). This second list may be filled with people from the next step.

- To find new contacts, you'll want to find networking events to go to. These are often on the MeetUp website, and you can also find sessions at most conferences where you can network.

- Make an action plan. For each list, make a checklist or spreadsheet. At least once a week, set aside 30 minutes to reach out.

- Reach-out plan. Many of your activities might be over LinkedIn. Realize that people get a lot of spam messages on LinkedIn of people trying to sell them things. Be different. Do a little research on the person. Have they posted recently? Is any new job activity listed? Then, start your approach from an attitude of wanting to serve them. Instead of being a taker, be a giver. Your message can be simple and light - "Hey, Awesome Person - Love your post on X. It reminded me of the time we did Y. Hey, I would love to catch up for 20 minutes and hear what you are up to now. Are you free on (specific time here) for a quick chat?"

- On the chat - listen and hear the person out. People like to talk about what they are doing. Jot down notes of ways you could help them. If it makes sense, bring those up. After hearing them chat, if there's time, mention something you'd love help with. Keep it short.

- Follow-up in 24 hours with a short message thanking them for chatting. If you have the action items you took from the chat, share those.

- Update your checklist or spreadsheet often. While you don't want to be annoying, you may need to follow up every few weeks to get a response. People are super busy and forget.

These steps sound simple, and they honestly haven't changed that much from the non-digital age. Yes, now it is easier to reach-out, book time, and meet online. However, the people side of networking remains the same. Make a connection, hear them out, help them, then ask for help. Later, they may have an inside connection with a place you are looking to interview.

One way to get this done is to gamify it. Make it a challenge. Find a friend to do this with and commit to doing it for four weeks. Touch base with your friend every week on your progress. Like working out, it's a lot easier to get motivated when we are accountable to someone else than going it alone. Also, you could gamify this with some weekly or monthly reward you do with your friend - or maybe even the people you network with.

CHAPTER 39

Skill – Confront the BS Head On

"Cats don't have to work very hard to be cats. It comes pretty naturally to them. But, for us as human beings, we have to work very hard to be human."

— Simon Sinek

"Why not just call out the BSer on their BS?" asked one of my colleagues when I asked their thoughts on this book. "Letting them get away with it is most of the problem."

It's a fair point. If there weren't BSers, we wouldn't have BS to deal with. How many times have you played a movie in your head where you tell that BSer at your work off? Did it look like a scene in the movie? Did theme music play, and was there a victory dance afterward? How many times have you seen it go down like that in your life?

For most of us, there's a dichotomy here - what we think we really want to say and what we do. There are often cultural norms and acting can be stifled by the fear of repercussions.

But what if some direct communication, in addition to skill building, could be part of the solution? With all the emotion pent up around this, what's the best way to get a result and not get caught in an everlasting shitstorm?

However, some experts have approaches for this that can help. In addition to the skills you have learned, there's a timing part to consider. You may have to wait until things have calmed down and are not so heated. You may need a safe environment and even permission to bring things up. You may need to do some research and be prepared with multiple ideas in advance. Perhaps the hardest part to accept is that you may have to actually give a crap about what the BSer has to say to you.

We will go over three approaches here that have science and an evidence-based approach behind them. While other approaches might feel or sound good on paper, these are proven. The three approaches are "FBI" from Simon Sinek, "OTFD" from Quantum Learning and "CPS" from Lives in the Balance.

FBI

"There is an entire section in the bookshop called self-help, but what we really need is a section called Help Others." — *Simon Sinek*

Simon Sinek has many exceptional books and lectures worth checking out. (78)

One of the approaches that he created is called "FBI". No, this is not an interrogation technique, but it is a way to structure conversations to get more positive results and avoid dancing around a topic. (79) Like all these approaches, the setup is important. This is best done in a 1-1 or small group conversation. It's great to say upfront something like, "I'd like to talk to you about something pretty difficult - is that ok?" And yes, you do want and need their buy-in here for this to work. You will then walk through the FBI framework, and it's good to have done some of this in advance to be prepared with some notes:

F - Feelings

State your feelings clearly and avoid words like "always" and other generalizations. Feelings are usually a couple of words here, like sad, mad, glad, frustrated. If your feelings are multiple sentences, those are thoughts and other things. Your limbic system, where emotions thrive, has no sense of language, remember?

B - Behavior

Talk about the behavior that triggered the emotions (or vice versa). This would be something someone watching a video of the event would also say happened. Be careful to avoid biases as much as you can.

I - Impact

This is where you bring up the consequences of leaving this situation unaddressed and your desire to help things change with their help. If you have any facts or figures here, that can greatly help focus the discussion instead of going to a battle of perspectives.

Yes, this can be a challenging conversation to have. However, the beauty of it is that you get to have it once instead of hundreds of times a week to yourself. An article sharing this approach reminds us "By embracing discomfort, we open doors for deeper connections and conflict resolution." (80)

OTFD

Expressing ourselves objectively, when we have emotions tied to it, can seem almost impossible. In these cases, some structure makes it a lot easier. This will help you communicate what's going on so that others can get it and some positive action can occur.

This approach comes from Learning Forum and its award-winning programs for teens and adults. (81) Over four decades, they have led programs all over the world with their evidence-based, practical tools to help people learn and thrive. Full disclosure: I have a bias because their programs changed my life for the better. I was fortunate enough to be a student of their programs in the 1980s. I was also on their staff team later. I have many lifelong friends thanks to the amazing founders Bobbi and Joe.

One of the powerful approaches their programs teach has the acronym OTFD, or the pneumonic "Out The Front Door". It's a great tool to express anything and ask for action, and easy to use.

O - Observation

This is where you start, and you own your perspective. It sounds something like, "I noticed that this happened." Stick to what others might call facts here and avoid interpretations. We'll get there.

T - Thought

After sharing your observation, it's time to talk about what you made up about it. We all make things up about events, it's how our brain works. This sounds something like, "and I thought that you didn't like me." We have to be brave, honest and vulnerable here for this to work.

F- Feeling

Okay, now we go to feelings. Again, these are a few short words, not sentences. Sentences are thoughts. This sounds something like, "and I was mad" or "I felt hurt".

D- Desire

And now, we ask for what we want. This can be a big step for us. Sometimes, we don't ask for what we want out of fear, and then we are surprised that it doesn't show up. This sounds like, "and I'd like to figure out how we can get along better."

For OTFD, let's dive into a quick example. Let's say you were in a meeting with some people, and a peer got upset about something. You might agree with them, but it may have come across stronger than you would have delivered it. Others on your team may have been intimidated by the tone or not understand the complexity of the topic.

You find time to chat with your colleague in the next few days. This is a live conversation - not email or chat. Here's what that could sound like with the OTFD framework:

"Hey Cutter, thanks for meeting. I wanted to chat about something with you. Is that okay?"

"Yeah, sure, Billy Bob, what's up?"

"Yeah, so in that HR meeting the other day, it seemed like that topic about having a quota for performance for your team was tough to swallow. I observed you having a lot of energy and some very strong counterpoints."

"Yeah, that really pissed me off."

"Yep, got it. Let me go through a few things really quickly if that's okay."

"Sure, buddy."

"Thanks, so when I heard that, I made up that you were angry at HR and didn't like them. I also made up that you wanted to fight about it with them."

"Oh, dude, I didn't mean it that way."

"Yep, hang on, amigo, just want to complete something here."

"Got it, go ahead."

"So, I felt a little sad. I thought others might not see your brilliance because they may be afraid of direct communication."

[Yes, this example combines feelings and thoughts, which may happen. It also packages each to be clear.]

"So, what I'd love to happen is to figure out a way to support you, man. You have great ideas, and maybe just packaging them differently would give a different approach. In those moments that get hot, how can I help?"

For this hypothetical situation, notice there was no blame, there was a lot of ownership, and the presenter asked politely to finish. They also asked for action and offered to help. The structure also makes it easy to stay on task and not get stuck in a quagmire of stories and emotions. A partnership is formed, and actions and support are to be taken together.

This approach, like the others, may take a few rounds before things move. Remember the trimtab example - you are moving a tanker, and tankers don't like changes in direction. It will take focused and repetitive actions for change to happen. This can be hard when we have pent-up anxiety and frustration and want immediate relief. If it helps, remember how you react when people ask you to change. Do you always do it and go? Or do you resist it and justify how you are fine as-is? Most of us do the second thing, and it takes time for us to accept and adopt.

Okay, let's move on to the last approach for dealing with things directly.

CPS

"The definition of insanity is doing the same thing over and over again and expecting a different result."

[This quote is attributed to Albert Einstein, Benjamin Franklin, and George Bernard Shaw. Imagine what those three could talk about!]

Let's get something out here first. While I love this approach, the acronym is the same as Child Protective Services, which can be triggering. Luckily, in this case, CPS stands for Collaborative & Proactive Solutions from Dr. Ross Greene and his Lives in the Balance organization (82). Dr. Ross Greene has created and refined this approach over many decades. Others have done similar and complementary work, including Dr. Stuart Ablon and Dr. Bruce Perry. In this book, I'm going to focus on Dr. Greene's work primarily.

Now, on first blush, this approach might not make total sense in the workplace. To be clear, Dr. Greene's organization describes this approach as "is the evidence-based, trauma-informed, neurodiversity affirming model of care that helps caregivers focus on identifying the problems that are causing concerning behaviors in kids and solving those problems collaboratively and proactively."

Now, normally, the work situation isn't like a parental or school one, right?

We don't have behavior issues, diversity issues, different perspectives or things not working out with old approaches, right?

Of course, we do. My first exposure to this, however, was working with my son, who is on the autism spectrum. That's another book - literally (*Unleashed: What a Child With Autism Can Teach You*). Later, I realized this approach worked with everyone - because we all have the same brain wiring. Yes, other more sophisticated studies (than my n of 1) have shared the same results. Now, to really become adept at this, I recommend checking out Lives in the Balance - Dr. Greene's website. There are a lot of videos and tools you can adopt right away.

I also want to preface this quick overview by saying I was probably the biggest skeptic when I started. This sounded way too touchy-feely, and I wanted results. In the case of parenting, I didn't want to collaborate, I wanted to be in charge. If that comes up for you at all, know that using this approach has made me convert my ways. And as a parent, I'm still able to have my parental expectations for my kiddo. This carries over to my work expectations as a leader. This isn't about settling or going for a mediocre result. It's about a better result than you can even expect now. The other thing to understand before we jump into the how is what science has shown to be true.

"Kids do well if they can... if this kid could be doing well, they would be doing well... if the kid isn't doing well, something must

be getting in the way. It's also the belief that we all do well if we can." – Dr. Ross Greene (83)

This is a big jump for many. We were brought up to believe that people fail because they don't put in enough effort or they must seek to be disruptive. We can believe that some people want to be assholes and spread BS.

For just a few paragraphs, do your best to let that go.

So, if people want to do well - and something is in their way for that to happen - how do we get it out of their way?

This is where the "Plan B" approach from Dr. Greene comes into play. Here are the steps in this plan.

1. **Empathy** - You may stay on this step for many days. This isn't about rushing to step three. There is no award for this. However, there can be major issues if you rush it. This step, you will actually listen, empathize and validate. You don't have to agree. You don't have to like it. You aren't giving a lecture. This sounds like, "Hey, this event seemed rough, what's going on?" After actively listening, you need to say back to them you understand that they feel that way - and it makes sense they feel that way. Again, you aren't agreeing, but you are acknowledging what's going on for them being real for them.

2. **Your Concern** - Only after the person has felt heard and validated do you move on. Here is where you share your concerns. And, sorry, it's short. That movie about telling someone off with the great monologue? That doesn't work here. You share your concern in a couple of sentences or less. This sounds like "My concern is safety." Then you ask

if they understand that concern. The first few times you do this, you may need to go back to empathy. That's okay. With empathy, you are unraveling knots and building trust.

3. **Problem-Solving** - Done with fidelity, this approach has now calmed things down considerably. The threat response mechanisms have chilled out, and adrenaline and cortisol are not feeding everyone a rage-stress cocktail anymore. The cortex can start problem-solving and collaborating. Imagination is able to flow more easily. While this approach will seem like magic after you do it, the results of this can be stunning. I have seen creative approaches I would never dream of come into play here. In this part of the model, only after empathy and concern are heard and understood, you ask the other person their ideas for fixing or addressing the issues. Wait what? What about what you want to happen? Hold on for a bit. You are going for a result here, not being right. And, if it comes from the other person, the chance of it sticking and lasting is considerably better. If it's your idea - it will always be your idea, not theirs, or yours. Now, you want to encourage brainstorming here. This means that some ideas aren't practical. That's okay. It's better to get a lot of ideas out there. This may also take a few times chatting, and you can come back to it. Once you have a number of ideas, all you need to do is decide between both of you what one you want to try out, and when you want to check-in about how it's going. Yes, you get a say here about which approach works for you, as the other party gets one about what works for them.

All too often, we jump to problem-solving. Unless we address how our brain works and use empathy and validation first, we'll get the same crappy results.

The other thing that happens here, and there are plenty of studies to back this up, is that the person who struggles is actively building up skills. Instead of the same neuropathways that are creating BS, they have new ones to start using. While we have around 80-100 billion brain cells, we have 100 trillion connections. There are nearly endless possibilities for new paths to be formed, and we don't have to stay stuck.

Wrapping Up

You now have three approaches to address charged situations instead of charging right in and playing your "I was right" and "I was wronged" dialogue. While that dialogue is great for your screenplay, the reviews for that in the workplace are seldom positive. These approaches require us to take different actions than we are used to. Because of that, I highly recommend that you focus on the result you are looking for, as well as your why.

SECTION SIX

How do you use this?

Understand how to best apply what you have learned for your success.

CHAPTER 40

Formulas and Tools

"Relax, all right? My old man is a television repairman, he's got this ultimate set of tools. I can fix it."

— *Jeff Spicoli, Fast Times at Ridgemont High*

Earlier in the book, I suggested treating these tools and ideas like a buffet - taking what made sense to you and maybe trying a little bit of something new here and there. Now you have some new tools. So, as Jeff Spicoli suggests above, you may be able to fix anything - or at least, many things. While you can use the buffet mindset as your approach, let's also talk about using the best tool for the job.

"If the only tool you have is a hammer, it is tempting to treat everything as if it were a nail."

— *Abraham Maslow*

Now, you may have lots of nails to deal with at your work, and likely you also have a few screws loose (figuratively). You may have bolts to loosen (or tighten), things to saw, structures to level, and even things to duct tape. So, let's talk through a few approaches to decide your best tool choices.

1. <u>Practice With Each Tool</u> - This is contrary to the buffet world. This more may be of the notion to "eat everything on your plate." To build competency in using new tools, you actually have to, well, use them. So, I recommend you at least attempt to use each tool at least three times. Yes, it will probably be awkward for some. The result here is that you may discover you can use the equivalent of a Sawzall instead of a craft knife and get better results.

2. <u>Ideate Your Approach</u> - Now you have some expertise in a variety of tools, you'll want to brainstorm on your approach. You can do this by yourself or with someone you trust. One easy way to do this is to write down each tool on a Post-it. Then, write down your situation on another Post-it. Put that on a wall or desk, and then attach tools you think will work.

3. <u>Combinations Are Okay</u> - Unlike physical tools or food, mashups are okay here. You may use a couple of the tools here. These are normally used at different times to get incremental progress or based on feedback of how these work. If you get stuck in wondering if X or Y should be used, use both.

4. <u>De-brief</u> - This is often missed in the workplace and in our growth. One of my work colleagues told me that when he was a rescue diver in the Coast Guard (yes, he was a badass), they would have a "hot wash" after missions. The team would wash the helicopter together, inside and out. As they did that, they would talk about what worked well and what didn't. You can use this same approach, no helicopter required. And yes, you may need to talk out loud to yourself to do this. Reflect on what went especially well, what

changes you might make next time, and congratulate yourself on a successful mission. Even if it feels like a mess, you are making progress and moving forward.

Just Winging It

It can feel great to just wing it or go with the flow. From a musician's perspective, improvising and jamming can be satisfying. Being in the moment, in the zone, and doing whatever comes to us is a great place to be.

Using that same perspective, musicians spend countless hours memorizing chords, learning drills, and playing many types of music to be a great improviser. They also listen - a lot - to other successful musicians. And, all the time, they are playing off of them - or better put, figuring out how to play their own stuff, but in harmony with the group.

Much like that musician, you can get to the place where you can improvise, be in the zone and jam with your anti-BS instruments. Before you can rock on with your bad self, please take the time to do your scales and drills. It won't take that much time, and you'll enjoy much better results. Like a musician, you'll have to take things slow to get them down well. Sometimes it won't sound so good and may even be embarrassing. But the next time, you'll have it down a lot better.

And no matter how rough it is at first, keep at it as consistently as you know how to. The tunes you play - your unique brilliance - is greatly needed in the world. While I wish you didn't have to wade through BS to get it out there - we all do. Equipped with a few practiced approaches, we'll all be able to hear, see and experience what you have to share, so much easier.

CHAPTER 41

Are You The Asshole?

Much of this book is written for those who feel that BS is being done to them, and they need relief from this. While that is true for just about everyone, maybe you are the asshole sometimes.

I know, how dare I. There's no possible way you are the asshole.

Or is there?

Stay with me if you can, even if this pisses you off.

Most of our brains will play top hits of how we are right, and someone else is totally in the wrong. That's how we are wired, and it is frankly normal. It's a simple program.

But what if, without trying to be (of course), we are being assholes? What if we said or did something that created a shitshow for someone else?

Spoiler alert - if you are breathing, that likely has happened.

This is tricky for me sometimes because I'd love to think that all of my faults are forgivable. And instead, those who do things "to me" are villains for life. So dramatic and righteous, right?

There are always outliers. There are people who are experts at BS creation, and it is hard to use tools to help reduce the spread. There are few of these on the planet, thank goodness, and they are toxic. It's highly unlikely that you are one of them.

However, there's this middle ground where most of us have moments when we don't have the skills to handle a situation, and we spread BS. We may be great people, but we are also BS spreaders. Some people may only know us for that. That's the only dimension they have.

What if - and I know it's a stretch - what if the person or situation creating crap for you also has another side to it. It is so hard to believe or see when we are literally covered in it. But what if that had the slightest possibility? What if?

Now, the work to get there might not be for us. No doubt. We might not have the interest or energy after being covered in crap. But what if someone else reached them and reduced the flow of crap?

I mention this because, in our direct interactions, it may well be just too much for us to handle. Forgive yourself; you don't need to be a saint and walking away from junk can be the smartest play. Here's the nuance though - in situations you aren't directly in, can you be the person bringing out the best in the person who struggles? Can you help encourage colleagues, peers, and leaders - in situations that aren't so charged - to refrain from BS?

And, if enough of us do this, it starts to create a fabric where the BS spread isn't a sure thing. Using the skills in this book might even put it in check.

So yes, at times, I know I've been the asshole at work. I sure didn't intend that, and when I reflect on it, I would handle things differently. I do now. But then, I clearly created BS for someone to have resilience around. If you are one of those people and I haven't apologized for this already, I'm truly sorry. Please let me know how to make it up to you.

For you reading this, the other lesson to learn here is that we might need to give people a bit of a break. This doesn't excuse their behavior or things done but acknowledges that they might honestly be clueless. And, without someone cluing them in, change is not likely. While they might not admit it, maybe they are scared shitless. Maybe they had brutality in their life and haven't yet dealt with that trauma. Maybe they are exposed to things you aren't, and their decisions don't make sense.

And maybe their job is not to have you be delighted with everything in the workplace. Whoa.

Part of the resilience building is to reflect on this, check in with our why, use our tools, and keep going.

The best news is that when you have an asshole moment, it means you are human (sorry, aliens, I'm not sure of your asshole capabilities). Expecting - of yourself or others - perfect composure is absolute BS. We are literally not wired that way. We have natural emotional cocktails that can take us over for a time due to no fault of our own. While we owe it to ourselves and everyone to limit those and learn skills to function, it doesn't take away the human imperfections.

And when we have those asshole moments, we don't need to stay stuck there.

Forgive yourself. Let it go, choose different actions and move on.

CHAPTER 42

Best Practices for BS Reduction Routines

As it turns out, we need some routines and repetition to make success in BS reduction. Just having it sit around doesn't lead to growth and, frankly, creates a cesspool of problems.

Breaking up the patterns - yes, those greatest hits in our RAS - takes some consistent effort and check-ins. Fortunately, this work is honestly light and rarely hurts.

Here are a few routines I recommend to help you on your BS resilience journey:

- After practicing each tool a few times, note which ones are more natural and easier for you. Also, note if some had more surprising results than you expected.

- Where and when possible, help others out of their BS. This doesn't need to be some giant counseling session - just simple things like, "Hey, let's do our next 1-1 walking around the park". For my remote working friends, this can easily be done on your devices, too. In addition to helping reduce the BS spread at your work, the act of serving and helping others is a stress reducer for yourself.

- Create a simple one-year plan for your BS reduction at work. On that plan, have 3-5 goals for the year and create a few milestones each quarter. Track your progress on the first or last day of each month and make adjustments.

- Consider a workbook or journal to help your progress. With a few minutes a day, you can see significantly more progress than blazing through a book and hopping to the next one. Often, we need a reminder to get us back on track or to consider other ideas. You can do this with the exercises in this book, a blank journal of your choosing, or the optional workbook paired with this book (easily found on Amazon).
- Consider an accountability buddy. This can be an in-person or online friend you check in with regularly. The act of checking in helps most of us stay in action and keep helping those excuses. Most of us are exceptional excuse creators - too busy, too tired, other commitments, and other excuses. When we know that "Gees, I need to tell my friend on Monday where I'm at on this," we're more likely to stay on task.
- See what your workplace offers or plans to offer. With the uptake in wellness awareness at many corporations, there are often new programs to help reduce stress and increase productivity. In addition to direct benefits, you may find yourself connected to others who want BS reduction and are acting on it.
- After a major milestone or after a year, plan a celebration for yourself. In this, you are actually recognizing achievement here and not just celebrating to celebrate. It's important to acknowledge yourself. It's a challenge to build this resilience and rise above the autopilot so many of us are on. One great way to do this is to book a massage, spa treatment, or something else that is restorative to you.

Finally, do your best to unfixate on work BS. This is absolutely the hardest for me. Most of my first conversations with my wife after the workday were about BS. I still struggle with that as a go-to. And, while it's important to connect, why the heck would I wish all that BS on her? Usually, it's because I haven't packaged it up (skill), am overwhelmed and don't know what to do with it, or honestly, most likely - bad habit.

When I'm retired, I know I'm unlikely to say - "gees, I wish I complained more about work BS." So, the more I can let that go - and take action - the better. While we're both tired after work, conversations about "what fun thing are we going to do next" are a lot more interesting than some crap story about a lame coworker or incompetent leader.

CHAPTER 43

Congratulations!

Wow. You did it. You made a major step to increasing your BS resilience and reducing the amount that you have to deal with. Reading this book is a step so many may miss. Instead of enjoying the greatest hits they pick, they'll be stuck with the BS blues.

Our human spirit and potential are phenomenal. So many things get in the way of this, and when we let it shine through, the outcomes we all enjoy are simply exceptional. While work is, well, work and maybe not always the most fun endeavor we dream of, it also doesn't have to suck all the time. There are also times when it is challenging, and that doesn't need to consume us. There's a balance here, and I hope this book helps you find it.

Our expectations of our workplace, and sometimes our government, have become interesting, too. It's more common to expect to have things done for us instead of being directly involved in serving others. And there's an upset that can happen when this attitude of "serve me" doesn't result in our exact needs being met. When it comes down to it, only we are capable of totally understanding and finding ways to meet our needs. Attempts by others, however noble, will have some shortcomings. This doesn't mean we're an island and can't ask for help, but it also doesn't mean that the world and workplace and our government owe us. They don't.

While living our passions and sharing our gifts is important, the road to that may be filled with things we don't love doing or don't love doing for a time. This doesn't mean we aren't living our passion, but it does mean that we'll appreciate the goal and may learn something along the way. The effort, or proof of work, gives value to what we achieve. Without some notion of this, the value is greatly diminished.

This also isn't about putting up with a bunch of crap forever. While short-term or episodic is one thing, we owe it to ourselves to take action to reduce the workplace BS, change it, or leave it. What can be hard about ping-ponging around is that we may be making the same choices, failing to build the needed skills, and repeating the BS at many employers. Having done this, I can tell you it's exhausting.

And, as much as the workplace is about someone or something else, it's also about us.

"It's me, hi, I'm the problem, it's me"

— Taylor Swift

While uncomfortable, there is usually some part of us that is a part of a BS workplace solution. While that might feel like it sucks, it also rules. It means we can take action and change it, and don't have to sit in it.

Sometimes, these situations are complex, and the solutions aren't obvious. Using a couple of the tools, maybe on the smaller issues, will create relief and the space for other actions.

As a final note, be careful about distractions as a coping tool. We have many devices and opportunities for instant digital entertainment. It's easy to get hooked on that dopamine rush. As much as you can, make sure that you are using some of the other skills shared in this book as your coping and BS reduction techniques. Escape can be helpful, but if we don't make changes in what we are coming back to, we won't move forward.

Thank you so much for investing in yourself and reducing the BS in our workplaces. While it's not always easy, it's also not anywhere close to impossible. More importantly, the world needs your brilliance, creativity and gifts to be shared.

There are so many possibilities for your career journey that haven't yet been explored, and there's no need to be or feel stuck. The timing sometimes isn't instant, and it's also not never.

It's there.

As my favorite coach once told my skeptical self, "Just be open to the possibilities!"

Use your smartphone camera to click below, or just go to **thebsbook.com** for extra tools, tips, and trainings!

Thank You

Thank you so much for buying and reading this book! I greatly appreciate your time, energy, and investment in yourself. My avid intent is for this book to serve you.

In writing this, I have a massive list of people to thank and appreciate. My direct style and passion can create a world of problems. Early in my career, a friendly leader nicknamed me "clean up, aisle seven."

Being neurodivergent, my brain also goes in about twelve directions at once and fast. It is interesting to engage with me as my cortex is combining seemingly unrelated things in a conversation. Linear is not something that I do, which is hard for logic-lovers.

I've also made big and dumb mistakes and have created BS in the workplace. It wasn't some big evil ploy but being unaware and having a huge blind spot.

Luckily, I've also had phenomenal coaches, programs, and life lessons to help me along the way. Some of these were structured programs, and others were little subtle coaching ideas. Both of those are mentioned in this book.

I'm especially thankful for the people who have seen me for who I am and who I intend to be. Those are really the best people in our lives, right? The ones who can see past our own BS and know what we are about.

Here, that's certainly my wife, Cathie. It's also the rest of my family, including my awesome son Cooper and Penelope, the wonder pup. Thank you all for both putting up with me and giving me a chance to shine! Thank you for accepting my apologies when I screw up.

I also have a long list of professionals to thank. My career has been blessed with some great leaders, colleagues, and coaches who have also seen me for who I am. To protect their privacy, I will not call them out. However, they will read this, smile, and nod, and they will know which stories honor them. Thank you!

Bibliography

1. Women, work, stress, and heart disease: 5 ways to protect yourself. Harvard Health. (2011, February 15). https://www.health.harvard.edu/healthbeat/women-work-stress-and-heart-disease-5-ways-to-protect-yourself

2. Lloyd-Jones, D., Adams, R., Brown, T., Carnethon, M., Dai, S., & Simone, G. (2009, December 17). Heart Disease and Stroke Statistics—2010 Update. Heart Disease and Stroke Statistics. https://www.ahajournals.org/doi/10.1161/CIRCULATIONAHA.109.192667

3. Hundrup, Y. A., Simonsen, M. K., & Obel, E. B. (2011, March 18). Cohort profile: The Danish nurse cohort. OUP Academic. https://academic.oup.com/ije/article/41/5/1241/706209

4. Liu, X., Liu, C., Schenck, H., Yi, X., Wang, H., & Shi, X. (2017, December). The risk factors of 9-year follow-up on hypertension in middle-aged people in Tujia-nationality settlement of China. Journal of human hypertension. https://www.ncbi.nlm.nih.gov/pmc/articles/PMC5680414/

5. Women, work, stress, and heart disease: 5 ways to protect yourself. Harvard Health. (2011a, February 15). https://www.health.harvard.edu/healthbeat/women-work-stress-and-heart-disease-5-ways-to-protect-yourself#:~:text=When%20the%20fight%2Dor%2Dflight,can%20trigger%20a%20heart%20attack.

6. Stressed, sad, and anxious: A snapshot of the global workforce. Harvard Business Review. (2022, June 15). https://hbr.org/2022/06/stressed-sad-and-anxious-a-snapshot-of-the-global-workforce

7. Perceptions of construction work: Views to consider to improve employee ... (n.d.). https://ascelibrary.org/doi/10.1061/%28ASCE%29CO.1943-7862.0002057

8. The neurobiology - pcaiowa.org. (n.d.-b). https://pcaiowa.org/content/uploads/2019/02/neurobiology-of-stress-report.pdf

9. Job stress health effects: Total worker health for employers: CPH-New: Research. Total Worker Health for Employers | CPH-NEW | Research | UMass Lowell. (n.d.). https://www.uml.edu/research/cph-new/worker/stress-at-work/health-effects.aspx

10. By: Marina Martin and Updated: 03-26-2016, By: Marina Martin and, and, M. M., & 03-26-2016, U. (n.d.). How inefficiency negatively impacts your business. dummies. https://www.dummies.com/article/business-careers-money/business/operations/how-inefficiency-negatively-impacts-your-business-169146/

11. Bridging the document disconnect in sales - adobe. (n.d.-a). https://esign.adobe.com/rs/345-TTI-184/images/idc-bridging-the-document-disconnect-sales.pdf

12. Networking statistics everyone should know (2024). Apollo Technical LLC. (2023, January 17). https://www.apollotechnical.com/networking-

statistics/#:~:text=In%20fact%2C%20according%20to%20CNBC,that%20recruiters%20meet%20through%20networking.

13. Adkins, A. (2023, July 21). Millennials: The job-hopping generation. Gallup.com. https://www.gallup.com/workplace/231587/millennials-job-hopping-generation.aspx

14. Ivanova, I. (2023, September 5). Millennials didn't kill the "organization man" after all. Federal Data reveals it was the boomers all along. Fortune. https://fortune.com/2023/09/02/job-hopping-millennials-boomers-switching-careers-disloyalty-organization-man-bls/

15. Arain, M., Haque, M., Johal, L., Mathur, P., Nel, W., Rais, A., Sandhu, R., & Sharma, S. (2013). Maturation of the adolescent brain. Neuropsychiatric disease and treatment. https://www.ncbi.nlm.nih.gov/pmc/articles/PMC3621648/#:~:text=The%20development%20and%20maturation%20of%20the%20prefrontal%20cortex%20occurs%20primarily,helps%20accomplish%20executive%20brain%20functions.

16. Forbes Magazine. (2023, December 27). New Year's resolutions statistics 2024. Forbes. https://www.forbes.com/health/mind/new-years-resolutions-statistics/

17. Studies show 91 percent of Us won't achieve our New Year's ... (n.d.-c). https://www.inc.com/marcel-schwantes/studies-show-91-percent-of-us-wont-achieve-our-new-years-resolutions-how-to-be-9-percent-that-do.html

18. Shivali-Best. (2020, January 2). Day that people most likely to give up New Year's resolutions - and it's soon. The Mirror. https://www.mirror.co.uk/science/day-people-most-likely-give-21199904

19. Post. Outburst Rage Room. (n.d.). https://www.outburstrageroom.com/post/the-science-behind-why-breaking-things-can-be-therapeutic

20. Supasitthumrong, T. (2023, August 3). Endorphins - the "feel good" chemicals for well-being. MedPark Hospital. https://www.medparkhospital.com/en-US/lifestyles/endorphins#:~:text=pain%2Drelieving%20drug.-,Endorphins%20are%20neurotransmitters%20released%20by%20the%20pituitary%20gland%20and%20hypothalamus,exercise%2C%20and%20sex%2C%20etc.

21. Team, D. (2023, August 21). Catharsis: Its meaning and mental health benefits. Daisie Blog. https://blog.daisie.com/catharsis-its-meaning-and-mental-health-benefits/#:~:text=When%20you're%20faced%20with,that's%20where%20catharsis%20comes%20in.

22. Morgan, J. (2015, April 15). Why smaller teams are better than larger ones. Forbes. https://www.forbes.com/sites/jacobmorgan/2015/04/15/why-smaller-teams-are-better-than-larger-ones/?sh=355acb701e68

23. Administrator. (2016, January 22). Ringelmann effect - iresearchnet. Psychology.

https://psychology.iresearchnet.com/social-psychology/group/ringelmann-effect/

24. By, Hoffman, R., on, U., 7, S., & Riley Hoffman Lab Manager at Yale University B.A. (2023, September 7). Social loafing in psychology: Definition, examples & theory. Simply Psychology. https://www.simplypsychology.org/social-loafing.html

25. Mueller, J. (2018). Creative change: Why we resist it... how we can embrace it. Mariner Books.

26. Morgan, J. (2017, December 7). Why smaller teams are better than larger ones. HuffPost. https://www.huffpost.com/entry/why-smaller-teams-are-bet_b_7069616

27. Bradberry, T. (2023, November 18). How complaining rewires your brain for negativity. TalentSmartEQ. https://www.talentsmarteq.com/how-complaining-rewires-your-brain-for-negativity/#:~:text=Complaining%20triggers%20your%20body%20to,are%20essential%20to%20immediate%20survival.

28. Managing a chronic complainer. Harvard Business Review. (2021, September 1). https://hbr.org/2021/04/managing-a-chronic-complainer#:~:text=A%20continuous%20cycle%20of%20negative,black%2Dand%2Dwhite%20thinking.

29. The 8 keys of excellence - supercamp. (n.d.-d). https://www.supercamp.com/pdf/RS-2018-19-6-8-Keys-Speak-with-Good-Purpose.pdf

30. Rhodes, A. (n.d.). A brief summary of the long history of Risk Management. Ventiv Technology is now Riskonnect. https://www.ventivtech.com/blog/a-brief-summary-of-the-long-history-of-risk-management

31. Group, I. (n.d.). Risk management market size, share, trends, forecast 2024-2032. Size, Share, Trends, Forecast 2024-2032. https://www.imarcgroup.com/risk-management-market#:~:text=Market%20Overview%3A,13%25%20during%202024%2D2032.

32. Companies ranked by revenue - page 4. CompaniesMarketCap.com - companies ranked by market capitalization. (n.d.). https://companiesmarketcap.com/largest-companies-by-revenue/page/4/

33. Jason Firch, M. (2022, November 11). 10 cyber security trends you can't ignore in 2021. PurpleSec. https://purplesec.us/cyber-security-trends-2021/

34. The latest Cyber Crime Statistics (updated February 2024): Aag it support. AAG IT Services. (2024, February 1). https://aag-it.com/the-latest-cyber-crime-statistics/#:~:text=Since%202001%2C%20the%20victim%20count,standing%20in%202021%20at%20%24787%2C671.

35. Wikimedia Foundation. (2024, February 7). Kodak. Wikipedia. https://en.wikipedia.org/wiki/Kodak

36. Nfpa.org. (n.d.). https://www.nfpa.org/

37. U.S. National Library of Medicine. (n.d.). Home - PMC - NCBI. National Center for Biotechnology Information. https://www.ncbi.nlm.nih.gov/pmc/

38. Train your brain to be more creative. Harvard Business Review. (2021b, October 11). https://hbr.org/2021/06/train-your-brain-to-be-more-creative

39. Lee, J., Tsunetsugu, Y., Takayama, N., Park, B.-J., Li, Q., Song, C., Komatsu, M., Ikei, H., Tyrväinen, L., Kagawa, T., & Miyazaki, Y. (2014, February 10). Influence of forest therapy on cardiovascular relaxation in young adults. Evidence-Based Complementary and Alternative Medicine.
https://www.hindawi.com/journals/ecam/2014/834360/

40. Author links open overlay panelLiisa Tyrväinen a, a, b, c, d, AbstractThis study investigated the psychological (perceived restorativeness, Berg, A. E. van den, Frumkin, H., Hartig, T., Hartmann, P., Hellhammer, D. H., Herzog, T. R., Kirschbaum, C., Korpela, K., Kudielka, B. M., Laumann, K., Lee, J., Levine, A., Lovallo, W. R., … Kaplan, R. (2013, December 24). The influence of urban green environments on stress relief measures: A field experiment. Journal of Environmental Psychology.
https://www.sciencedirect.com/science/article/abs/pii/S0272494413000959

41. Stress recovery during exposure to natural and urban environments … (n.d.-c).
https://www.sciencedirect.com/science/article/abs/pii/S0272494405801847

42. Ricks, D. A. (2006). Blunders in international business. Blackwell Pub.

43. Merriam-Webster. (n.d.). Vent definition & meaning. Merriam-Webster. https://www.merriam-webster.com/dictionary/vent

44. The Role of Vents in Caps and Closures. Tri-Sure. (n.d.). https://www.tri-sure.com/news-events/the-role-of-vents-in-caps-and-closures

45. Wikimedia Foundation. (2024a, January 18). API. Wikipedia. https://en.wikipedia.org/wiki/API#:~:text=There%20are%20APIs%20for%20programming,until%20the%201960s%20and%201970s.

46. Wikimedia Foundation. (2024b, February 5). EDSAC. Wikipedia. https://en.wikipedia.org/wiki/EDSAC

47. Wilkes, M. V., & Wheeler, D. J. (1957). The preparation of programs for an Electronic Digital Computer. Addison-Wesley publishing.

48. Wikimedia Foundation. (2024a, January 18). American Federation of Information Processing Societies. Wikipedia. https://en.wikipedia.org/wiki/American_Federation_of_Information_Processing_Societies

49. Kerner, S. M., & Burke, J. (2021, May 6). What is FTP? file transfer protocol explained. Networking. https://www.techtarget.com/searchnetworking/definition/File-Transfer-Protocol-

FTP#:~:text=The%20first%20specification%20for%20FTP,the%20precursor%20to%20the%20internet.

50. Wikimedia Foundation. (2023, October 5). ANSI-SPARC architecture. Wikipedia. https://en.wikipedia.org/wiki/ANSI-SPARC_Architecture

51. Goebelbecker, E. (2019, January 10). Service oriented architecture: A dead simple explanation - dzone. dzone.com. https://dzone.com/articles/service-oriented-architecture-a-dead-simple-explan

52. Gillis, A. S. (2020, September 22). What is Rest Api (restful API)?. App Architecture. https://www.techtarget.com/searchapparchitecture/definition/RESTful-API#:~:text=History%20of%20RESTful%20APIs&text=In%202000%2C%20Roy%20Fielding%20and,the%20University%20of%20California%2C%20Irvine.

53. Martin, S. (2024, February 1). Microservices. Wikipedia. https://en.wikipedia.org/wiki/Microservices

54. WebMD. (n.d.). Signs of guilt: Obsessive-compulsive disorder, depression, physical symptoms, and overcoming excessive guilt. WebMD. https://www.webmd.com/mental-health/signs-guilt

55. Gupta, R., Koscik, T. R., Bechara, A., & Tranel, D. (2011, March). The amygdala and decision-making. Neuropsychologia. https://www.ncbi.nlm.nih.gov/pmc/articles/PMC3032808/

56. Slattery, A. (2020, July 29). How to handle brown-nosing & the rise of Ingratiation. InHerSight. https://www.inhersight.com/blog/insight-commentary/brown-nosing-at-work#:~:text=in%20psychology%20and%20is%20an,not%20immune%20to%20its%20charms.

57. The Science of Visualization: How to encourage positive thinking and goal achievement. RSS. (n.d.). https://www.corporatewellnessmagazine.com/article/the-science-of-visualization-how-to-encourage-positive-thinking-and-goal-achievement#:~:text=Studies%20have%20shown%20that%20visualization,attention%2C%20concentration%2C%20and%20memory.

58. Visual image reconstruction from human brain activity using a ... (n.d.-g). http://www.cell.com/neuron/fulltext/S0896-6273(08)00958-6?_returnURL=http%3A%2F%2Flinkinghub.elsevier.com%2Fretrieve%2Fpii%2FS0896627308009586%3Fshowall&cc=y

59. Munroe-Chandler, K. J., & Guerrero, M. D. (2017, April 26). Psychological imagery in sport and performance. Oxford Research Encyclopedia of Psychology. https://oxfordre.com/psychology/display/10.1093/acrefore/9780190236557.001.0001/acrefore-9780190236557-e-228

60. Massa Mohamed Ali, Hbs. C. (2022, May 24). The science of Visualization: Can imagining your goals make you more likely to accomplish them?. Neurovine.

https://www.neurovine.ai/blog/the-science-of-visualization-can-imagining-your-goals-make-you-more-likely-to-accomplish-them

61. Ranganathan VK;Siemionow V;Liu JZ;Sahgal V;Yue GH; (n.d.). From mental power to muscle power--gaining strength by using the mind. Neuropsychologia. https://pubmed.ncbi.nlm.nih.gov/14998709/

62. The Playboy interview February 1972. (n.d.-g). https://www.bfi.org/wp-content/uploads/2022/02/CandidConversation-Playboy.pdf

63. Greene, R. (n.d.). Lives In The Balance. https://livesinthebalance.org/

64. Lindner, J. (2023, December 16). Must-know work ethics statistics [recent analysis] • gitnux. GITNUX. https://gitnux.org/work-ethics-statistics/

65. Jameslopresti. (2023, November 27). 5 biggest ethical issues facing businesses - Florida tech online. Online Degrees - Florida Institute of Technology | Florida Tech Online. https://www.floridatechonline.com/blog/business/the-5-biggest-ethical-issues-facing-businesses/

66. 2018 Global Business Ethics Survey®. Ethics & Compliance Initiative. (2021, October 25). https://www.ethics.org/knowledge-center/2018-gbes-2/

67. 15 biggest compliance fines ($1billion and above). Data Privacy Compliance Software for Apps, Websites, & SaaS.

(2024, February 10). https://www.enzuzo.com/blog/biggest-compliance-fines

68. EEOC releases fiscal year 2018 enforcement and Litigation Data. US EEOC. (n.d.). https://www.eeoc.gov/newsroom/eeoc-releases-fiscal-year-2018-enforcement-and-litigation-data

69. Caregivers in the workplace - worklife law. (n.d.-b). https://worklifelaw.org/publications/Caregivers-in-the-Workplace-FRD-update-2016.pdf

70. Safety and Health at Work (Safety and Health at Work). Safety and health at work (Safety and health at work). (n.d.). https://www.ilo.org/global/topics/safety-and-health-at-work/lang--en/index.htm

71. U.S. Bureau of Labor Statistics. (n.d.). IIF Home. U.S. Bureau of Labor Statistics. https://www.bls.gov/iif/#:~:text=There%20were%205%2C486%20fatal%20work,per%20100%2C000%20FTE%20in%202021.

72. What is the uncertainty principle and why is it important?. Caltech Science Exchange. (n.d.). https://scienceexchange.caltech.edu/topics/quantum-science-explained/uncertainty-principle#:~:text=Formulated%20by%20the%20German%20physicist,about%20its%20speed%20and%20vice

73. Knowledge does not protect against illusory truth. (n.d.-c). https://www.apa.org/pubs/journals/features/xge-0000098.pdf

74. https://www.buzzwordbingogame.com/cards/buzzword/

75. Adler, L. (2020, August 18). New survey reveals 85% of all jobs are filled via networking. LinkedIn. https://www.linkedin.com/pulse/new-survey-reveals-85-all-jobs-filled-via-networking-lou-adler/?trk=Yahoo_News

76. Julia Freeland Fisher, director of education research at the C. C. I. (2020, February 14). How to get a job often comes down to one elite personal asset, and many people still don't realize it. CNBC. https://www.cnbc.com/2019/12/27/how-to-get-a-job-often-comes-down-to-one-elite-personal-asset.html

77. Eighty-percent of professionals consider networking important to career success. LinkedIn Pressroom. (2017, June 22). https://news.linkedin.com/2017/6/eighty-percent-of-professionals-consider-networking-important-to-career-success

78. Sinek, S. (n.d.). Leadership Training & Employee Development Platform. Simon Sinek. https://simonsinek.com/

79. Sinek, S. (2023, July 10). Try this the next time you have an uncomfortable conversation | Simon Sinek. YouTube. https://www.youtube.com/watch?v=RcGkHrPSzDc&t=162s

80. Gooijer, M. de. (2023, July 16). Simon Sinek on how to best have uncomfortable (but important) conversations. BrightVibes. https://www.brightvibes.com/simon-sinek-on-how-to-best-have-uncomfortable-but-important-conversations/

81. SuperCamp, a world-wide program. SuperCamp. (2022, September 30). https://www.supercamp.com/

82. Different lenses, different practices, and different outcomes. LIVES IN THE BALANCE. (n.d.). https://livesinthebalance.org/our-solution/

83. Greene, R. (n.d.-b). Lives in the balance. Lives In the Balance. https://vimeo.com/user15771052

Disclaimers

All the names, situations, companies, and accounts in this book are fictional. While they are based on actual events that the author or his colleagues have experienced, many details and names have been changed.

Because of these situations being commonplace, one may think they know of a specific incident being referenced. However, great care was taken to protect specific companies, people, and situations. None of the accounts refer to a specific organization or event to protect all parties. None of the names, other than that of the author, are real names in these encounters. Further, all accounts in this book have had fictional components added to better make a point or help the reader understand a topic.

No trade or company secrets were used or leveraged to create this book. Any perceptions of events are those of the author. There is no intent to slander or misrepresent any of his past, present or future employers. The author appreciates all the things his employers have taught him. Please wear sunscreen.

www.ingramcontent.com/pod-product-compliance
Lightning Source LLC
LaVergne TN
LVHW051823080426
835512LV00018B/2695